AN INTRODUCTION TO 11TH STEP MEDITATION:
MEDITATION:
RECOVERY AND INSIGHT

An Introduction to 11th Step Meditation: Recovery and Insight

by

Laurence Sanger

ISBN 978-1492706724

102513

Insights Publishing Company
Dallas, Texas

Dedication

To Mike, for being there when it counted.

To Choicemakers and Preston, for fellowship.

To my Dharma teachers, who generously share what they are learning.

To Mary, for bringing such unexpected joy.

11th Step

Sought through prayer and meditation to improve our conscious contact with God, *as we understood Him*, praying only for knowledge of His will for us and the power to carry that out.

Maybe there's something else to life than just getting what you want all the time…That something else is finding the joy within oneself, rather than as a result of life circumstances.

—Cheri Huber

 I think all of us are like eagles who have forgotten that we know how to fly.

—Pema Chödrön

To arrive where you are, to get from where you are not,
    You must go by a way wherein there is no ecstasy.
In order to arrive at what you do not know
    You must go by a way which is the way of ignorance.
In order to possess what you do not possess
    You must go by the way of dispossession.
In order to arrive at what you are not
    You must go through the way in which you are not.
And what you do not know is the only thing you know.
And what you own is what you do not own.
And where you are is where you are not.

—T.S. Eliot

Contents

Preface

For years I've dreamed of writing a book. My excuse for not doing so has been, "I have nothing to write about." Well, now I do.

The topic at one particular 12-Step meeting was the 11th Step. As usual when the 11th Step was discussed, most people shared their experience, strength (or struggles), and hope c o n c e r n i n g prayer and their Higher Power. Nobody mentioned meditation until the very end of the meeting, when a woman spoke a little about it. While sharing she commented that meditation was one of the most undeveloped subjects in 12-Step Programs. I remember thinking, "I certainly agree with that. It's too bad there's no 12-Step Program meditation literature. In fact, I could…".

Bingo! Suddenly it all came together for me at that meeting. I could write a book about 11th Step and meditation.

How could I qualify to write such a book? I've been in recovery including meditating daily, since December 1991. Although I'm not an expert, I certainly have lived intimately with this discipline since then. Meditation has been the single most powerful 12-Step recovery tool for me, with the possible exception of attending 12-Step meetings on a regular basis. I have been continually perplexed and disappointed that meditation is rarely discussed — barely even mentioned — in the thousands of 12-Step meetings I've attended. Program literature contains few references to meditation; most of those references confuse meditation with prayer. Occasionally I have mentioned meditation in meetings and with friends in recovery but it has rarely sparked any discussion or interest. Mostly it drew blank stares.

The 11th Step *"suggests"* that in addition to prayer we meditate. Everyone in recovery knows something about how to pray; our 12 Steps and literature even suggest *what* to pray. But relatively few in recovery seem to know how to meditate.

An Introduction to 11th Step Meditation: Recovery and Insight is about meditation in the context of the 12 Steps. It assumes you are or have been in a 12-Step program, or at least that you are curious about 12-Step recovery. It also assumes you would like to learn something about how meditation fits into a 12-Step program. This book is not a thorough or scholarly treatment of the subject; it's an introduction. The Endnotes at the end of this book contains several good books on the subject of meditation, all except a couple of which are completely outside the context of 12-Step recovery.

This book is divided into three parts:

- Part One *My Story*, tells how I came into 12-Step recovery and discovered the power and value of an 11th Step meditation practice.

- Part Two *Meditation*, discusses meditation with detailed instructions on a simple but powerful meditation practice.

- Part Three *Meditation and the Program*, sketches how meditation relates to and enhances a 12-Step Program.

By sharing my experience and some of what I have learned meditating within the context of a 12-Step Program, I hope this book will answer the following main questions:

- What is meditation?

- How do I meditate?

- How does meditation work in a 12-Step Program?

- How can I develop a consistent meditation practice?

I hope this book will encourage you to learn more about meditation. Most of all, especially for those of you in recovery, my wish is that you give meditation a genuine try to discover for yourself how a meditation practice can enhance and accelerate your recovery.

I have a strong belief that meditation is a priceless but woefully underused recovery tool, easily accessible to everyone in the Program, no matter what your religious beliefs. I also believe that meditation is equally valuable to those who are not in recovery but who want to live a saner, wiser and more serene life. I sincerely hope you will find something of value for your recovery here. As always in recovery, with this book, take what you like and leave the rest.

--LS

Part One
My Story

CHAPTER 1

My Story

"Hi, my name is Laurence. I'm a grateful member of this Program."

If that sounds familiar to you, you probably are or have been a member of a 12-Step Program.

If you are new to 12-Step recovery, or have never been in recovery, let me explain what it means for a member to tell his "story." From time to time, a 12-Step Program member is asked to tell the members of his home group or another 12-Step group an abbreviated autobiography generally designed to fit into an hour and to cover the following topics in a general way:

- what he used to be like (before he came into a 12-Step Program)

- what happened (to cause him to become involved in a 12-Step Program)

- what he is like now (since he has been in a 12-Step Program)

This chapter briefly sketches my story, modified to cover these three topics to emphasize the beginning of my experience with an 11th Step meditation practice.

What I Used to Be Like.

I was born in Dallas to an upper middle class nonobservant Jewish family. I received a fine liberal arts education, culminating in a law degree in 1973. The intellect — learning, education and knowledge — was the pinnacle of my value system.

My mother used and abused alcohol and prescription medications while I was growing up. From her forties onwards she suffered from an undiagnosed and untreated anxiety disorder, which for her meant generalized anxiety and specific phobias like driving, flying, elevators and being alone. Mother drank to allay her fears, but alcohol only exacerbated them. She had only enough emotional energy to maintain appearances for Dad and her social devoirs and to keep her drinking and emotions reasonably in check. There just wasn't much left in her for nurturing my brother or me.

Dad made some effort to control Mother's drinking, but naturally he was unsuccessful. Partly generational and partly inherent in his character, Dad was a somewhat distant parent. His parenting style was often judgmental, critical and blaming. Appearances and what "the neighbors" thought were of highest consequence to him. With his message "don't draw attention to yourself," my brother and I learned not to be, not to show, and not to know who we really were.

My parents, especially my father, constantly judged, compared, classified, rated and ranked my (and everyone's) actions, feelings and thoughts, often against a blurry idea of conforming to "What You Should Do" and "How It Will Look" so it would not spoil "Your Permanent Record." A difference of opinion meant someone had to be right (and win) and someone had to be wrong (and lose), even if these opinions were only matters of personal taste and opinion.

Our home life was quiet — a little too much so. The atmosphere was emotionally cool and a bit antiseptic, as if everyone were just going through the motions. Big emotions were rarely expressed directly, with the chief exception being my outbursts of angry or rebellious behavior.

A clear and present danger was usually involved in exposing my true feelings and thoughts. Because my parents were often subtly shaming about my feelings and thoughts, I learned to keep them secret. I did this by denying, minimizing or intellectualizing my feelings and concealing my thoughts. No wonder I grew up emotionally immature and haunted by my own unacknowledged or unexpressed feelings and thoughts. To protect myself against the threat of what I perceived to be a fearsome, judging and hostile world, I became often somewhat defensive and defended, aggressive, sarcastic, judgmental, indirect and manipulative.

Our home was non-spiritual. Discussion of God, the nature of world, Reality, Truth or the Meaning of Life just did not interest my parents. God was like a book-of-the-month club selection that was shelved on arrival in the mail, unread.

During the summer of 1967, when I was 20, I began to smoke marijuana. Within a few months I was smoking grass daily. Perhaps this is controversial, but marijuana and later LSD were introduced to me as spiritual tools and sacraments.

My closest friends and I smoked marijuana, and later took stronger psychedelics like LSD, for spiritual reasons, at least at first. By using these psychedelic ("mind-manifesting") substances, we attempted to transcend the ordinary, day-to-day material world and enter the realm of direct experience of a Higher Power we commonly called "Cosmic Consciousness." My spiritual context was a very rudimentary understanding of Eastern religions, primarily Hinduism, Taoism and Buddhism, as "interpreted" by such heroes as Timothy Leary, Ram Das, and Alan Watts. By comparison, the religion of my youth seemed an empty shell of ritual and rules. But these Asian spiritual traditions — they were *alive and ablaze with meaning and wonder.* Their spiritual texts such as the Bhagavad Gita, Tao Te Ching, the Vedas and The Tibetan Book of the Dead mapped out in precise detail practical spiritual paths — including meditation — successfully walked for more than fifty centuries. The metaphors and descriptions in these ancient writings closely corresponded to what we hippies were experiencing when we "turned on." My blending of Asian spiritual principles and psychedelics earned me the name "Acid Monk" in 1968.

It would be considerably euphemistic to write that I "experimented with drugs" in the late '60's, but I did not wear a white lab coat and there was certainly no peer review. For two or three years, however, I did conduct informal experiments in consciousness alteration and I did have this hypothesis: psychedelic drugs tore away the veil of routine perception, awakening a conscious contact with a power greater than myself, a Higher Self or Cosmic Consciousness. I considered myself an "experimental chemical theologian" as I searched for the Truth.

As part of this journey I took LSD about fifteen times in 1967 and 1968. My first acid trip was a life-transforming event. I had an intense spiritual experience of the first magnitude, a burning bush encounter with what I then called the Clear Light of Reality and I now consider a Higher Power. It is incapable of description. However, when the experience ended, I recall saying in awe, "So this is what all the saints, poets and philosophers are talking about!" I had a peek at Heaven. An irony is that at the time I thought I could replicate the experience at will. This assumption was as wrong as I have ever been. My 13th acid trip was a ticket to a terrifying cartoonish Hell Realm. It was a bad trip of the first magnitude. I cannot adequately describe the terror of that long night in 1968, but it has remained imprinted in my nervous system and my mind to this day. I had a peek at Hell.

Following my Bad Acid Trip, I occasionally began to experience anxiety when I was high on grass. In 1968, I abandoned LSD as just too strong and too anxiety producing. This decision caused me considerable shame because I felt I was somehow unworthy of direct spiritual experience. I continued to smoke grass daily but what began as "turning on" eventually became just "getting high," often alone in apartments with locked doors and drawn shades. I continued to read about Asian religions, but mainly as a mere intellectual involvement. Eventually what had begun as a vital spiritual journey deteriorated into a cul-de-sac of routine, self-deception, compulsion, arrested maturity, greed and fear.

After graduating from college in 1969, I worked a few months in a downtown Dallas bookstore and continued to smoke grass daily. I fell in with a small group of men and women about my age who were "devotees" of an Indian guru none of us had ever met. We smoked grass, chanted and meditated together; we read lots of the same spiritual books; and we talked and talked and talked about karma, reincarnation and the Meaning of Life.

It was about this time that we met a local Dallas spiritual teacher whose approach seemed to conform to ours. One afternoon, a few months after meeting this teacher, I received a phone call that the teacher would "initiate" some of us that day! This was very exciting, although exactly what we were being initiated *into* was not clear. We had a brief preliminary ceremony, with meditation and chanting. Then it was time to be initiated. A line formed in front of the teacher, who spoke in turn to each of us some quiet words and completed the initiation by placing a finger on our Third Eye and pressed firmly. (The Third Eye is the supposed nonphysical eye of spiritual awakening, located just above the eyes in the center of the forehead.) By pressing on our Third Eye, a Spiritual Awakening evidenced by a powerful internal White Light was supposed to occur. Wowie zowie! Come on down!

When it was my turn, I moved to the teacher and stood in front of him. He softly spoke into my ear and then placed his finger on my Third Eye and pressed.

"Do you see It?" he asked.

"Oh, yes," I said.

I was initiated! Hot damn!

This was a life-changing moment. Why? Not because I was now initiated. Not because of any radiant White Light. No, my life changed because I lied. I told the teacher (and later my friends) that I had seen "It," the White Light, when in fact I hadn't seen much of anything. I wanted so much to be initiated, to be one of the elite spiritual few, that I lied about the most important thing in my life — my own spiritual truth. I gladly donned the Emperor's New Clothes.

Soon I quit my job at the bookstore and moved to San Francisco with friends. The most vivid San Francisco memory I have is regularly going into my bedroom closet in the townhouse where we lived, high on grass, to meditate in the dark. In this closet I had set up a simple altar on which I placed my plaster statute of the serenely meditating Buddha (which I had bought at a liquor store). I had painted the Buddha's raised Third Eye with yellow phosphorescent paint, so that it glowed in the dark. Trying to meditate in a closet, high on grass and staring at a glowing Third Eye has come to represent the degraded state of my spiritual life by that time — I was going through the motions, but it was all superficial, a mere light show of the mind. Somehow I had almost entirely lost any substantial conscious contact with a Higher Power.

After a few months in San Francisco, I enrolled in law school. I had stopped meditating by the time I arrived back in Austin for law school, and gradually, imperceptibly, one day at a time, my vital spiritual experiences became pleasant but empty memories. Over the next several months, I drifted away from anything but a passing thought of a Higher Power and a spiritual connection. One afternoon in 1972 while reflecting on what had happened to my spiritual life, I admitted to myself that I had laid aside my spiritual search, but I intuited that perhaps in twenty or thirty years I would pick it up again. I was right about that. Recovery has taught me that spiritual experience, no matter how profound, requires regular and delicate nurturing or else it transforms from a living experience into a desiccated fossil.

In 1973 I graduated from law school and began my career as a lawyer by day and grass smoker by night. Since about 1970 I had felt occasional anxiety when I smoked grass but that only slowed my use down a little. One morning in 1975 I was in Ft. Worth in a Judge's chambers for a pretrial motion when I began to have panicky feelings. This was the first time I had ever experienced anxiety and panic when I was not high on grass or some other drug. It was very frightening. This anxiety attack was so upsetting that within a few weeks I stopped smoking grass forever.

I experienced my second serious panic attack in 1976. My lunch companion mentioned someone recently had put LSD in the mustard at the restaurant where we ate, resulting in serious panic among the patrons. My "what if" thinking quickly plunged me into sickening, overwhelming fear that it had happened to me! This was a profoundly traumatic experience. A legacy of this episode was that having a panic attack and LSD were somehow inextricably linked in my mind. Each panic attack I have had in the years since then and even moderate anxiety episodes (and there have been plenty) has caused me to wonder if I were just having an "ordinary" panic attack or if I had somehow been slipped LSD. You can see why admitting insanity was easy for me when I came in the doors of my first 12-Step Program.

In 1980 I married Claudia. We were both immature and our marriage plainly reflected that. I had not used drugs since 1975 and, perhaps turned off by my mother's abuse, I never cared for alcohol. Claudia had used drugs and alcohol for some years before we married. When we married, she was not using drugs but she did continue to drink alcohol.

Early in our marriage, Claudia and I took a brief course in Transcendental Meditation, but we were never able to develop any kind of consistent practice and soon abandoned it.

Claudia and I began snorting cocaine in 1982, a quite popular self-destructive activity at the time. Soon serious marital problems developed. After about three months, I quit using cocaine. I just stopped. This was not difficult at all, which is why I do not think I qualify for Alcoholics Anonymous or Narcotics Anonymous. Claudia continued to use secretly for a time but she stopped a few months later.

The most significant consequence of my brief cocaine abuse was that the frequency, intensity and duration of anxiety and panic attacks began to increase. For instance, during a vacation tour of the White House, I suddenly felt panicky — *I had to get out of there*. The fear subsided, but two days later as Claudia and I were about to take off on our flight back to Dallas, I began having another panic attack and got off the airplane just before it took off. I made a life decision a few minutes after we deplaned. Watching the airplane taxi away, I remember thinking (and on an unconscious level, deciding) that from then on I would live with an anxiety disorder. I know this sounds nuts. Why would anyone choose this? Ask some of the therapists I have seen since; they don't know either. I later realized that frying my nervous system with a drug like cocaine was total lunacy, especially for those like me with genetic, learned, and psychological predispositions to anxiety disorder. I did not get back on an airplane for seventeen years.

Once back in Dallas, I was in denial about what had happened in Washington, definitely unwilling to face it. I was ashamed, confused and afraid. For weeks I was unable to bring myself to do anything about my fears. Finally, I began a long, expensive process of going to a series of therapists of various kinds. It didn't help much because I never even got near to my core issues with these therapists and, frankly, they were not very knowledgeable about anxiety disorders.

Unnoticed by me, Claudia's drinking increased after we returned from Washington. Maybe somehow the Washington vacation made us each realize our marriage was not working and we both started looking for a way out. Claudia chose alcohol, recovery and an affair. I chose an anxiety disorder, avoidance and shutting down emotionally.

One day in 1984, Claudia suddenly announced that she was an alcoholic/addict and that she had joined Alcoholics Anonymous. I was dumbfounded. "What? She doesn't even drink that much, does she? Why would she join AA? She's no more an alcoholic than Mother." I just didn't get it. Claudia began her recovery in AA, which continued during the remainder of our marriage. She went to lots of AA meetings, worked hard at her Program, developed a close group of recovering AA friends and began living an AA recovery life.

At Claudia's suggestion I attended some 12-Step meetings for spouses of alcoholics in 1984, but it just wasn't for me. For one thing, the powerlessness and unmanageability of the 1st Step made absolutely no sense to me then, because *I* was not powerless over alcohol – *Claudia* was. She was the one with the problem, not me. If anyone was talking about alcoholism being a *family* disease, I never heard a word of it.

Looking back from the perspective of over a dozen years, I can appreciate Claudia's involvement in AA was also a precious gift for me — my exposure to the 12 Steps from attending some 12-Step meetings, listening to Claudia and her AA friends talk about the Program, and living with a recovering alcoholic who was serious about her Program. I learned something about the 12-Steps, the slogans, the principles, the Big Book and How It Works. I never worked a Program then, but the seed was planted. It took a lot of fertilizer over several years before that garden began to bloom.

Like many with codependency issues, I had resentfully given away much of my power and identity to Claudia and our marriage. In some sense, I made them my Higher Power. I drifted away from old friends and former enjoyments as my life became increasingly narrow. I focused on my law practice and my home life. I was supportive of Claudia's involvement in AA, but I kept asking, "What about us?" I never realized I should also have been asking, "What about me?" When Claudia told me her recovery was her Number One priority, more important even than our marriage, I thought it was just talk. I had not even bothered considering what *my* Number One priority was.

By the fall of 1985, Claudia was spending more and more time with her AA friends, at meetings, step studies and other AA activities. She was also in community college, so she was away from home quite a bit. Even so, in September her absences increased and some of her behavior grew increasingly out of character and strange. To make a painful story short, in October 1985, Claudia admitted she had been having an affair with an AA friend.

I was devastated, confused, angry, betrayed, sad, scared. We tried marriage counseling in a last-ditch effort to save the marriage, but that failed. In January 1986, she moved out; by March 1986, after being sober for little more than eighteen months, Claudia and I divorced.

The next six months were the most painful of my life. For five years after divorce, I went through the motions, sleepwalking through life, defended on the outside and withering on the inside. Intimacy was a very rare commodity in my life then, although I did have one long-term relationship. I had absolutely no conscious contact with a Higher Power. The spirituality of the 60's and early 70's was only a memory.

My anxiety disorder was well-entrenched by this time. Many people in recovery can relate to an irrational fear of impending doom, but my version was a bit extreme. The episodes of intense, desperate panic attacks occurred, but they were not common — only once a month or so. But in the meantime I lived in almost constant fear of having panic attacks. Fear of fear itself. I became hypervigilant, always on the lookout for the smallest sign that a panic attack might be triggered. Onset of panic attacks shared several psychological characteristics with my Bad Acid Trip, so this made matters worse. My world continued to shrink because of an inexorable fear/avoidance cycle. For instance, if I became anxious in a tall building, I began to fear and avoid elevators and tall buildings. If I experienced a scare at a particular restaurant, I stopped going there. I became afraid to travel far from home. I avoided crowded places.

My worst fear, one I could not tell anyone, was that somehow a panic attack would leave me permanently insane and consigned to insane asylum where I would be drugged out of awareness and completely dependent on others. Actually, I already *was* insane; I just didn't know it. My career suffered because I was not emotionally strong enough to be an ambitious attorney. Like my Mother, I had enough emotional energy to keep up appearances, but not for very much else.

At age 44, I was confused, angry, isolated, afraid, essentially dead in spirit, living a life without meaning or purpose.

What Happened.

During a routine annual physical exam in 1991, my doctor questioned me about my anxiety disorder and I told her nothing had changed. She suggested anti-anxiety medication, which I reluctantly began to use. I desperately hoped my panic attacks would finally cease. Luckily, no such luck.

One day in November 1991, after starting the anti-anxiety medication, while having lunch with a friend and the woman with whom I was living, I experienced another panic attack. Damn! *Again.* After lunch I returned to my law office and shut my door, despondent and hopelessness about ever getting any better. I had been living with constant fear for over six years. Would I have this anxiety disorder for *the rest of my life*? What the hell was wrong with me? I slumped down onto my office floor, tears in my eyes. I was at my wit's end. This was my emotional bottom.

"What else can I do?" I thought. "I've exercised regularly to work off anxieties; that hasn't helped. I've seen a psychoanalyst three times a week; that hasn't helped. Now I'm taking anti-anxiety medication and *that* isn't helping. I've tried everything I can think of and nothing helps. I don't know what else to do. I'm just powerless over this anxiety disorder."

Powerless? Wait. *Powerless*? Wasn't "powerless" what they talked about in Step 1 of the 12 Steps? The recovery seed began to sprout. "Powerless" seemed so fitting, so *appropriate*. Something in the word "powerless" resonated deeply within me. I did not have a problem with alcohol, but I was definitely powerless over my emotional condition which derived from growing up in an alcoholic home and from my own drug abuse. I did not think AA was appropriate for me, but I wondered if there was a 12-Step Program that *could* help me.

At that moment, which in retrospect was the first time I took Step 1 ("admitted we were powerless" and that "our lives had become unmanageable"), I reached out for help. This was the first time I took Step 2 (came to believe that "a power greater than myself *could* restore me to sanity".) I phoned a lifelong friend, Mike, who had gone into AA just before Claudia. He was familiar with my anxiety disorder and my family history. In tears, I told Mike what was happening and asked if he thought a 12-Step Program might help with my anxiety disorder. Mike suggested I try a particular 12-Step program for adults from alcoholic families. On December 7, 1991, I attended my first 12-Step meeting.

What I'm Like Now.

I immediately took to the Program. Finding 12-Step recovery was like finding my original home for first time. I was soon attending meetings three times a week, quite easy because my first 12-Step group just happened to meet at a recreation center around the corner from my house.

Three realizations crystallized for me during my first year or so in recovery.

1.   I realized I was no longer alone or so different from everyone else. There were people in recovery who understood my problems as few others could. All I had to do was admit my powerlessness and reach out to others.

2.   I realized I had a right to all my feelings and thoughts, even the ones that were driving me nuts. Many people coming into recovery are reluctant to accept the idea of being "restored to sanity" because it implies they are "insane." It wasn't difficult for me at all. Hell, my anxiety disorder had its own classification number in the DSM (*Diagnostic and Statistical Manual of Mental Disorders*). As I kept going to meetings, reading the literature, talking to fellows in recovery, and making a first effort to work the Steps, I saw that I was actually *afraid of many of my own feelings and thoughts*. I feared my feelings and thoughts would be so overwhelming that they would annihilate me or literally drive me insane.

As I began to work the Program, I learned about the effects of alcoholism and growing up in an alcoholic, dysfunctional home. I began to see with increasing clarity that I had grown up hiding, denying and stuffing many of my feelings and thoughts because I was told, or at least I felt, they were inappropriate or wrong. It was no coincidence that my own feelings and thoughts that now plagued me. Unresolved thoughts and feelings do not die; they're just buried alive. We have all seen enough horror movies to know that eventually the monster will dig itself out of its grave and take revenge on those who buried it.

I saw there was nothing inherently wrong with my fears, anger, sadness, guilt, and shame. They are not character defects. What *was* wrong (problem-sustaining, not problem-solving) and what *was* a character defect was how I denied or unmercifully judged these feelings and thoughts rather than accept them. I learned I had to accept my feelings and thoughts before I could get beyond them and begin to heal.

As I began to understand the *causes* of my insanity — my family of origin; a genetic predisposition; and a witch's brew of drugs that I chose to put into my body — these very causes diminished in importance. Having some understanding of how I developed my anxiety disorder was necessary for me, but I did not just want to be a "well-informed" prisoner. I wanted out.

3.   I realized I could change my feelings and thoughts by changing how I acted. I could change! How many people r e a l l y know that we can change? The 12-Step Program, which is a spiritual program based on *action*, suggested specific tools to do just exactly that. I discovered I had some choice about what I felt and thought; and I had a great deal of choice about my attitude about what I felt and thought. And this all had to do with the action I took, over which I had control, although that control was often clumsy. But making these changes would require connection with a power greater than myself. How to do that?

By early 1992, I was attending several 12-Step meetings each week on a regular basis. I was reading the literature. I was involved in a Step Study group I organized. I was working the Steps. I was motivated. I was making friends. I was beginning to open up. I was feeling better. I was hopeful.

After a Saturday morning meeting in March 1992, I was talking with a woman who mentioned she meditated as part of working the Steps. This was a life-changing moment. Patty was the first person I heard speak about meditating as part of working the Steps. Regrettably, she was one of the few.

Of course I had seen the word "meditation" in the 11ᵗʰ Step over the previous months in recovery. At this point, I had just starting to work the Steps. I was not even close to being through formally working Step 1 the first time, much less focusing on Step 11. Still, as I walked home from the Saturday meeting, I wondered if I could meditate. After all, I had meditated sporadically in the late 60's, the early 70's, and in the early 80's and considered those efforts to be failures. How could I meditate now, knowing how hard it was for me before?

Over the next few weeks it became increasingly clear *why* I had "failed" at meditating before. I couldn't concentrate very well and my mind wandered away from the point of focus, no matter which type meditation I practiced. I was under the impression that "correct" and "successful" meditation meant remaining perfectly focused. *Not* remaining perfectly focused meant I was not doing it *correctly* or *perfectly*. Lack of perfection meant failure to me then. The fact that I was high on grass when I meditated (at least in the 60's) or that I did not really know what I was doing never occurred to me. Faced with failure, I had always done something I knew how to do perfectly — I quit meditating.

What was different in the spring of 1992 that encouraged me to give meditation another try? Well, for one thing, there it was, right there in the fifth word of the 11ᵗʰ Step — "meditation." If I was going to work *all* the Steps, I had to follow Bill W.'s "suggestion" to meditate. I read somewhere that the suggestion to work the 12 Steps is like the suggestion of a sky diving instructor who suggests his students wear a parachute when they jump out of the airplane. They don't have to follow the suggestion, but there are definite consequences if they don't.

A more fundamental difference encouraged me to give meditation another try. By four months into the Program, I was learning that I did not have to do everything — anything — perfectly. This involved redefinition of success and failure at a visceral level. I was beginning to see that my perfectionism only reinforced a self-defeating belief loop — I had to be perfect to be lovable; I could not be perfect; therefore, I could never be lovable. Now, I simply yearned to improve a little, one day at a time; that was enough for me. The Program was teaching me the principle of "progress, not perfection."

I began to comprehend that I inevitably *will* make mistakes because it is inherent in my human nature. When I make a mistake, the Program taught me to acknowledge it, accept it, take action to correct it, and move on, always move on. Perhaps there was something in this thinking that could apply to meditation. This was a critical breakthrough for me.

I had to overcome one final obstacle in making a decision to try meditating. What brought me into recovery in the first place was fear of many of my own feelings and thoughts. I had done everything I could think of to avoid facing them. Wouldn't meditation *force* me to face my feelings and thoughts on a direct and intimate level? Was I willing to do this? My intuition was that facing my feelings and thoughts in meditation was a place I had to visit on the road to recovery. I did not realize then meditation would become central to my life.

OK, so I was willing to give meditation a try. But which type of meditation? There were so many. It was all very confusing. I had some experience with several styles of meditation — Kriya Yoga, Transcendental Meditation (TM), a form of Hindu meditation. None of these styles really worked for me. After thinking it over, I decided what I wanted was a meditation style with three characteristics:

- simple

- non-religious

- consistent with the Program

With these considerations in mind, I did what I always do back then — I went to the bookstore. (This was before Amazon.com became available.) I found a book that described the theory and practice of most Eastern and Western approaches to meditation. I found a style of meditation that met the criteria I had established (simple, non-religious, Program-consistent) and that intrigued me — "insight meditation" (*vipassana*). This was a type of Buddhist meditation, but it did not require any particular *belief* or *dogma* to practice it. Its basic technique appeared in the meditation styles of many religions. Insight meditation promised a technique intended to awaken and improve what the 11th Step calls "conscious contact" with a Higher Power. What more could I want?

So it was that I began to develop an 11th Step meditation practice that has been crucial and life enhancing for me for many years.

Eventually I married Mary, a woman I knew from the Program. Best decision I ever made. Our wedding rings were engraved with

"One Day at a Time". We both try to apply the Program principles in all our affairs. Daily meditation practice remains a crucial part of my life.

The Program teaches that you can't keep it unless you give it away. A corollary is that unless you give it away, you don't have it.

> The devotee knelt to be initiated into discipleship. The guru whispered the sacred mantra into his ear, warning him not to reveal it to anyone.
>
> "What will happen if I do?" asked the devotee.
>
> Said the guru, "Anyone to whom you reveal the mantra will be liberated from the bondage of ignorance and suffering, but you yourself will be excluded from discipleship and suffer damnation."
>
> No sooner had he heard those words than the devotee rushed to the marketplace, collected a large crowd around him, and repeated the sacred mantra for all to hear.
>
> The other disciples later reported this to the guru and demanded that the devotee be expelled from the monastery for his disobedience.
>
> The guru smiled and said, "Oh, well, he's in a 12-Step program and he knows he can't keep it if he doesn't give it away."[1]

Part Two
Meditation

CHAPTER 2

Prayer and Meditation

> So what we're seeking is what's there when we stop
> doing everything else.
>
> —Cheri Huber

What *is* there when we stop doing everything else? That's what
meditation reveals and what is there can change your life.

The 11th step suggests two spiritual practices — prayer and
meditation — to improve conscious contact with our Higher Power.
If we use only one of these twin spiritual practices, prayer, we are like
the man who uses only one of his legs — he can still get around, but
not as easily or as fast as he could if he used both legs.

Even the most basic Program literature often confuses prayer
and meditation, giving the incorrect idea that prayer and meditation
are the same thing. They emphatically are not. ("In meditation, we
ask God what we should do about each specific matter."[2] "As
beginners in meditation, we might now reread this prayer very slowly,
savoring every word and trying to take in the deep meaning of each
phrase and idea."[3]) There are many styles of meditation, probably
thousands. But just because there are many styles of meditation does
not mean that anything and everything is meditation.

In meetings people sometimes say, "Prayer is talking to God,
meditation is listening to God." That adage hints at something of the
difference between prayer and meditation, especially if we realize that
"listening" is a special kind of listening, not with the ears but with a
full heart and an empty mind. (Interestingly, one Asian spiritual
tradition has only a single word for both heart and mind. This
demonstrates the intimate connection of the heart and mind; it also
shows the artificial Western distinction between the two.)

Prayer.

Prayer is direct address to a Higher Power. This address, which is a form of communication, can be either silent or spoken. Sometimes prayers are expressions of gratitude for something we have and appreciate — a special gift, the Program, material abundance, a beautiful warm spring day or a loving spouse. Sometimes our prayers are expressions of desire — health for a loved one, a new job, removal of a troubling character defect or guidance for a particular situation. Steps 7 and 11 speak to suggested subject matter of prayer.

Contemplation.

Contemplation, another spiritual practice not mentioned in the Steps, deserves brief mention for comparative purposes. Contemplation is concentrated silent reflection or thinking about a specific spiritual or religious idea, such as gratitude, love, acceptance, surrender or forgiveness. Our daily "meditation" books contain food for contemplative thought, but they are not books directly concerned with meditation.

Meditation.

Although we can easily describe prayer and contemplation, meditation is quite difficult to define because it is more an attitude of heart and mind with which most of us are only barely familiar (certainly on a conscious level) and for which there is not a generally understood or useful vocabulary in the West.

Meditation is utterly simple, so simple it cannot adequately be explained in words. We must experience it. That is why so many teachers and texts from all religious traditions necessarily use myths, parables, similes, metaphors and other symbols in trying to express what cannot be explained but must be experienced.

> Rather than try to create another state, simply allow
> space for whatever is going on.[4]

"Simply allow space for whatever is going on" may sound simple, but it isn't very helpful if you don't already know what it means. It is also life's hardest challenge to accomplish. Just try it.

Here are some other ways that meditation has been well described. Please read and reflect upon them.

What we frequently call formal meditation involves purposefully making a time for stopping all outward activity and cultivating stillness, with no agenda other than being fully present in each moment.[5]

Meditation has to do with opening what is closed in us, balancing what is reactive, and exploring and investigating what is hidden. That is the why of the practice. We practice to open, to balance, and to explore.[6]

Meditation is the only intentional, systematic human activity, which at bottom is about *not* trying to improve yourself or get anywhere else, but simply to realize where you already are.[7]

It is about stopping and being present, that is all.[8]

[Meditation is] . . . the art of conscious living.[9]

Meditation can be thought of as the art of awakening.[10]

The practice is to sit and let your heart become still and concentrated and then to use that concentration to examine the nature of the mind and body.[11]

Watch your own mind. Examine to see how feelings and thoughts come and go. Don't be attached to anything, just be mindful of whatever there is to see.[12]

In meditation, you deliberately set up conditions so that there is not much to do. It's a way of giving yourself the opportunity to watch what happens when you don't have a lot of things to do and a lot of things to occupy your time.[13]

Do these descriptions sound simple? Simple, perhaps, but surely not easy.

"Why, any child of three knows how to do that," said the student.

The teacher replied, "Any child of three may know how to do it, but even an eighty-year-old man finds it difficult to put it into practice."

Meditation also can be considered in terms of what it does. It develops qualities of a recovering mind and heart — for instance, relaxed alertness, attentiveness, waiting without expectation, intuitive listening, silent knowing, joy, openness, concentration, mindfulness, detachment, spaciousness, energy, courage, serenity, equanimity, wisdom, compassion, honesty, openmindedness, discipline, patience. Essentially meditation practice is "simply maintaining awareness — of our activities and of the thoughts that separate us from our activities."[14]

Shinzen Young, a meditation teacher I met one year, incisively described meditation as infusing any aspect of experience with the dual qualities of mindfulness and equanimity. True enough, but still, using words to explain meditation to a non-meditator is like trying to explain electricity to a lamp.

There are many styles of meditation. Part of my own recovery process has been finding and refining one that works for me. The type I practice, insight meditation (*vipassana*), aims at conscious development of present moment participatory awareness to cultivate calm, equanimity, wisdom and compassion. It is a simple and direct observation and experience of the nature of our mind/body process, our "Higher Self," our "Higher Power," or whatever term we may wish to use to describe the indescribable nature of what is.

We can think of insight meditation as consisting of two concurrent elements:

- concentration of the mind, which cultivates calm and tranquility

- investigation of the nature of reality (our Higher Power) through our mind/body process, which cultivates insight

There is an appropriate balance between concentration and wisdom, a balance that evolves as your meditation practice evolves. Concentration of the mind is like turning on a light switch; wisdom is the light that appears. If we want to light the room, we turn on the switch, but we don't continue to fiddle with the switch once the light is on.

These two elements, concentration and insight, cannot be separated, like two ends of a stick. Concentration is at one end of the stick; insight is at the other end. If you pick up the whole stick, both ends are lifted simultaneously. Where does concentration end and insight begin?

A useful analogy to understand meditation compares the mind to a lake that reflects the nearby forest. The lake's surface is calm or rough, depending on the weather and other conditions. As the wind picks up or rain falls into the lake, ripples or waves appear which distort or chop up the forest's reflection on the lake. When the lake is calm and waveless, the lake reflects the forest clearly. Likewise, when our minds are calm and there are few "thought-waves," our world is reflected clearly and conscious contact with our Higher Power improves. When the "wind of discursive thought"[15] disturbs our minds or when thought-waves such as anger, fear, greed or confusion rough up our minds, our perception of the world is distorted. Thought-waves degrade conscious contact with our Higher Power. When our minds are disturbed, we think, speak and act in ways we normally would not. Meditation is a process by which we calm our minds so that disturbing thought-waves are reduced, our perception of reality is clarified, and conscious contact with our Higher Power is improved. In a sense, meditation helps us "recover" our calm and serene mind and heart so that conscious contact with our Higher Power is realized. A regular meditation practice can

> free the mind from the distortions of self-centeredness, negativity, and confusions. Seeing life as a constantly changing process, one begins to accept pleasure and pain, fear and joy, and all aspects of life with increasing balance and equanimity. This balanced awareness, grounded in the present moment, leads to stillness and a growing understanding of the nature of life. Out of this seeing emerges wisdom and compassion.[16]

We must experience meditation, not explain it, because words cannot capture its essence.

The disciples were absorbed in a discussion of Lao-Tzu's dictum:

> *"Those who know do not say; those who say*
> *do not know."*

When the Master entered, they asked him what the words meant.

Said the Master, "Which of you knows the fragrance of a rose?"

All of them knew.

Then he said, "Put it into words."

All of them were silent.[17]

CHAPTER 3

Why Meditate?

Though gold dust is precious, when it gets into the
eyes, it clouds the vision.

—Rinzai

A sufficient reason to meditate is that the 11th Step suggests meditation
as part of a Program of recovery. If we are going to work *all* 12 Steps,
meditation will be part of our Program.

Step 11.

Steps 10, 11 and 12 have been called "maintenance Steps" because
working them maintains the progress and momentum we have
achieved in working Steps 1 through 9. These three Steps put the
practical spirituality of the Program into daily use.

The word "sought" in the 11th Step encourages us to engage in
an ongoing effort of daily prayer and meditation. Step 11 improves
our spiritual understanding of and relationship with the Higher
Power that is restoring us to sanity. The more we experience our
Higher Power through working the Program, the more sane we
become; the more sane we become, the more we want to experience
our Higher Power. Our entire meditation practice is the cultivation of
sanity.

Taking Our Medicine.

After we've been in the Program a while, we realize that the
"problem" which initially brought us to recovery (alcohol, drugs,

other people, gambling, sex, money, food, whatever) was only symptomatic of a deeper, spiritual disease. The Steps are the Program's prescription for curing that spiritual disease. Working all the Steps — including meditation — is taking our medicine. Since we are the spiritually sick ones, we cannot rely on our own judgment about which part of the medicine we will take and which we do not need.

Meditation helps us "recover" our true nature, which paradoxically was never totally lost "even in moments of delusion, nor is it gained at the moment of enlightenment."[18] We often hear in our 12-Step meetings that we are not human beings having a spiritual experience, but spiritual beings having a human experience. Meditation helps us see our spiritual nature, but also reveals that

> . . . if we pay close attention, sooner or later we see that there are no differences between "spiritual" and "human." We already are everything we yearn for.[19]

Outer World, Inner World.

Most of us spend a great deal of our time, effort and attention focused on that part of the world found *outside* us — the "outer world." This outer world focus is usually on some *activity*, either ours or someone else's, an activity that is occurring now ("I am so angry right now"), that happened in the past ("She once got roaring drunk in front of my parents"), or that may happen in the future ("They will fire me if I miss work one more time"). From an absolute point of view, no fundamental difference exists between the outer world and the inner world, but conventionally we think, talk and act as if there were.

The outer world activities with which we normally concern ourselves are commonplace — family, career, education, relationships, possessions, recreation. We love (or hate) to go to work, see a movie, eat at restaurants, watch or play sports, have sex, be involved in relationships, travel, create, shop. Ten thousand outer world activities are the focus of our lives.

If we find ourselves in recovery, we have tended to focus on troublesome activities in our outer world — alcoholics focus on getting and drinking alcohol; drug addicts focus on getting and using drugs; Al-Anons focus on getting the alcoholic or the addict to do or not to do what the Al-Anons think best; codependents focus on what others do or do not do; gamblers focus on playing and outcomes of games; sex addicts focus on getting and having sex; those with eating disorders focus on getting (or avoiding) and eating (or avoiding) food; and workaholics and "busy-aholics" focus on finding things to do and staying busy. This unbalanced obsessive and compulsive focus takes

> . . . our minds off our predicament, but in so doing they become addictive, perpetuating the very dissatisfaction they are sought after to alleviate.[20]

An inner world experience is always associated with what is happening in our outer world. When we first arrive at the doors of recovery, this inner world experience is often confused, superficial or vague. We may obsess about a beer, a joint, our alcoholic wife, our friend's life, the championship basketball game, the receptionist, a piece of chocolate cake or keeping up with our busy schedule. We may act out compulsively by drinking, drugging, controlling, gambling and so forth. These obsessions and compulsions, though often exciting, are actually numbing and distracting mental static we use to avoid facing our true feelings and the frightening truth of a pervasive dissatisfaction with our lives. Isn't numbing out or distraction at least partly why we obsess or act compulsively in the first place? Without help we cannot get at the root of the obsessions and compulsions to comprehend what is going on with us and to see ourselves as we really are. The very fact that we come into recovery and admit our powerlessness shows our willingness to surrender what hasn't worked for us, to let it go, and to open our hearts and minds to the possibility that there is a better way of living which *could* restore us to sanity. The Program and meditation help us do exactly that.

One way to understand the recovery process is that it realigns the primacy of outer world focus, balancing it with our inner world. As our recovery progresses, we gradually learn to increase our focus on, and understanding of, our inner world until a proper balance between the inner world and the outer world is achieved. We realize as we work the Program that the Steps are a road map for exploration of our inner selves *and* our inner world. How? In this context, the Steps encourage us to admit the things that preoccupy, disturb or harm (Step 1), to come to believe we *could* be restored to sanity by a "power greater than ourselves" (Step 2), to decide to "turn it over" to a Higher Power of our understanding (Step 3), to make and share a "moral inventory" (Steps 4 and 5), to have our character defects removed (Steps 6 and 7), to list and make amends to those we have harmed (Steps 8 and 9), to make a daily inventory and admit when we are wrong (Step 10), to pray and meditate (Step 11), and to work these Steps in all our affairs (Step 12).

Sooner or later if we are serious about recovery we find ourselves becoming crucially concerned with the inner world of our own character — courage, serenity, wisdom, honesty, openmindedness, discipline, patience, compassion, patience, honesty, open-mindedness, willingness, motives, habits, purpose — as we start to "change the things we can."

11ᵗʰ Step meditation deals directly, efficiently and powerfully in observing and then changing the landscape of our inner world and, consequently, our outer world. It helps us change the things we can.

Who Am I?

At least for *myself*, what I am seeking to recover is my true nature. This compels me to consider the question, "What *is* my true nature?" or more commonly, "Who am I?"

"Who am I?" Well, I cannot answer this question meaningfully, especially for someone else, but there is a point I want to make. We all have dozens, hundreds or thousands of roles, characteristics, and relationships that define us and create our identities. For instance

- I am my body — male, adult, 66 years old, balding

- I am my feelings — curious, happy, angry, worried

- I am my opinions — independent voter, alcoholism is a family disease, I love dogs and my dog, Spanky, is the best dog ever

- I am what I do — lawyer, meditator, reader, heart attack survivor

- I am what I own — car, house, books, a dog

- I am my relationships — husband, son, friend, law partner

We go through each day with a constantly shifting kaleidoscope of identities, depending on the changing circumstances of the outer world and the inner world. Meditation exposes who or what is the essence that *has* these roles, characteristics and relationships, what we *are* underneath them. Meditation creates an opportunity to de-role and experience the roleless self, the true person without rank, our true nature. Among other things, through meditation we gain context, objectivity, and the ability to detach. After we have meditated for a while, we see that our identities arise and pass away, ever-changing. Meditation is gradual *deprogramming* the persistent illusion of inherent value in and permanence of our identities.

The Big Book tells us, "First of all, we had to quit playing God."[21] Meditation is one way this becomes possible. For instance, somehow I assumed that what I have or want (a new car, that good-looking blond, a better job, happiness) can be "mine," that objects can be "mine," and that even I am "mine." The unholy trinity – "I," "me," "mine." Self-centeredness. If there is any belonging, it is we who belong to our Higher Power and not the other way around. We learn this in meditation when, for instance, we observe feelings and thoughts arise and pass away. When we have done this long enough, we realize that although we may create these feelings and thoughts, we can't control them and we don't own them; they come and go on their own. This realization flies directly in the face of one of our basic assumptions — that feelings and thoughts are "ours." The supreme addiction is our attachment to things being "me" or "mine". A wise person

> employs his mind as a mirror; it grasps nothing; it refuses nothing; it receives, but does not keep.[22]

Why Am I Doing This?

When it is time for me to practice daily meditation, once in a blue moon I wonder, "Now, *why* am I doing this meditation practice?" This is doubt. To challenge this unskillful thinking, I prepared a mental reminder list:

1. **Part of My Program**. Meditation practice is an action the 11th Step suggests. If I want to work all the Steps, I will meditate, just for today.

2. **Removes Doubt**. Doubt is a mind state that prevents me from being happy, joyous, and free. Not only will meditation dispel today's doubt, it will weaken my

tendency to succumb to such inhibiting doubt in the future.

3. **Practice.** If I get nothing else out of this meditation today, for 30 or 45 minutes I will practice patience, discipline and willingness.

4. **If Not Now, When?** If I do not practice the 11ᵗʰ Step today, here and now, when will I practice it? When do I need recovery if not now, this very moment?

Meditation provides a way for us to train in the middle way — in staying right on the spot. We are encouraged not to judge whatever arises in our mind. In fact, we are encouraged not to even grasp whatever arises in our mind. What we usually call good or bad we simply acknowledge as thinking, without all the usual drama that goes along with right and wrong. We are instructed to let the thoughts come and go as if touching a bubble with a feather. This straightforward discipline prepares us to stop struggling and discover a fresh, unbiased state of being.[23]

Sometimes I think of my Higher Power as being like the purloined letter of the Edgar Allan Poe story — invisible to me, yet right in front of my eyes all the time. I just wasn't looking in the right place.

The rabbi's grandson, Yechiel Michel, was playing hide and seek with another child. He hid himself for some time, but his playmate did not look for him. Little Yechiel ran to Rabbi Baruch and said amid tears: "He did not look for me!"

The Rabbi said, "This is also God's complaint, that we seek him not."[24]

CHAPTER 4

Meditation Misconceptions

There is a principle which is a bar against all information, which is proof against all arguments and which cannot fail to keep a man in everlasting ignorance — that principle is contempt prior to investigation.

—Herbert Spencer

When I have mentioned a meditation practice to people in recovery over the past few years, a common response I have gotten has been, "Oh, you mean sitting cross-legged with your eyes closed, holding your thumbs and forefingers together in a circle, and chanting 'Om'." Having stereotyped meditation based on a caricature, they can then dismiss one of the twin spiritual practices of the Program without thought. Obviously there are misconceptions about meditation, and perhaps I can clear up four of the most common ones.

Misconception 1: Meditation is Religious.

Although it is a spiritual practice, meditation does not belong to any particular religion any more than does prayer, joy or breathing. Meditation can be found in all religious traditions. It is even practiced by agnostics, atheists and nontheists. I believe meditation provides what many formalized and fundamental Western religions fear most — direct experience of a Higher Power without any required dogma, belief or intermediary. C.G. Jung wrote that formalized religion protects its members from direct experience of God, but this is what the 11th Step promises.

Misconception 2: Meditation is Weird.

Insight meditation, the simple, non-sectarian kind I discuss in this book, is not practiced to achieve some "altered state" — to go into a trance, have visions, develop psychic powers, have an out-of-the-body experience, or seek bliss. Certain meditation techniques do seek such experiences, but insight meditation is not remotely directed at them, which insight meditation teacher Jack Kornfield calls spiritual "Booby Prizes." Insight meditation is quite ordinary and seeks a grounded, in-the-body experience of the preciousness and truth of life, here and now, as it is in this very moment, just now. A refinement of 12-Step recovery's "One Day at a Time" principle, the present moment is the only place that truth exists; where else could it be?

Misconception 3: Meditation is Escaping Reality.

Meditation directly confronts reality, it does not escape it. When we meditate, we are as fully in the truth of the present moment as we can be.

What we are doing in meditation is the gradual dismantling of our complex deeply rooted denial and defense systems so we can see and experience our true nature as it is in this very moment. Like the Program itself, meditation is not running *away from* our problems, it is running *toward* them. It teaches us to stop, look and listen to our ordinary mind.

> Meditation is not world denying; the slowing down that it requires is in service of closer examination of the day-to-day mind. . . Its object is to question the true nature of the self and to end the production of self-created mental suffering.[25]

Misconception 4: Meditation is Selfish.

A 12-Step program is a selfish program in the sense that we each are working on ourselves to improve the quality of our lives. Until we begin to recover, how much help to others can we be? We only have to look at the chaos in our lives when we first came into recovery see how helpful we really were. Yet once we embark on our recovery journey, we realize we must be of service to others if we expect to maintain and develop our recovery. A Program adage is, "We can't keep it if we don't give it away." But an unspoken corollary to the adage is "We can't keep it if we don't have it in the first place." We can say the same of meditation practice. It is selfish in the sense we are exploring the truth of ourselves, but in that process we develop compassion greater than we have ever known before. "Let it begin with me." We do not practice for selfish reasons, but in order to improve our lives so that we can model that and be of service to others.

Misconception 5:
I Think Too Much to Meditate

"I can't meditate. My mind is just too busy!" Almost everyone faces this misconception when they begin meditating. But the point of meditation is not to stop thinking or to have an empty mind. It's true that as we progress in our meditation practice, the frequency, intensity and duration of our thoughts diminish, but this is an effect of meditation, not the goal. We meditate in order to change our relationship to our thoughts so that we can be happy, independent of what we are thinking or even what is happening in our external experience. The goal is closer contact with our Higher Power. I'll discuss this in more detail in Chapter 12 (Meditating with Thoughts).

Words are often totally inadequate to explain the essence of things, especially those things that are in plain view. Here is a story that reminds me of our tendency to misunderstand even the most obvious things:

> Once there was a spiritual teacher who was asked one night by his students to explain the moon to them. Realizing the limitation of words, the teacher simply pointed his finger at the moon. The students were amazed. "The moon is the Teacher's finger!"

CHAPTER 5

How Often, When and How Long?

> It's like putting a snake in a tube. For a little while, anyway, the snake cannot make a choice — it can only be straight.
>
> —Dainin Katagiri

How often, when and how long to meditate are entirely personal decisions that you'll make after trial and error. I encourage you to experiment. Remember, this is *your* meditation practice, just like it is *your* Program. The only area where I personally do not see much room for variation is my opinion that daily meditation is essential. Still, it is your Program.

How Often to Meditate?

How often you sit is up to you. However, consider this — if we are encouraged to pray every day, why wouldn't we meditate every day? For me, daily prayer and meditation are both indispensable elements of working the Program. Like tithing part of your income in some traditions, "tithing" part of your time, energy and attention to working your Program, including meditation, seems little enough to ask, especially when compared to the need for recovery and the results that await.

I practice formal meditation once each day, every day. Eventually I might practice twice daily (once in the morning and once at night), but at this point I am reluctant to risk burning out by overdoing it. For me, once is enough, but twice is too much right now. I practice meditation informally several times throughout the day.

When to Meditate?

I recommend that, if possible, you meditate at the same time or times each day. A regular schedule will act as an encouragement to your practice. The only time you might avoid meditation is just after meals, when you have a tendency to feel sleepy. Otherwise, any time is a good time. Experiment.

Practically speaking, early in the morning and last thing at night are generally quite conducive to the spiritual practice of meditation. Dawn and dusk are good times to bracket a busy day gracefully.

I am a morning person, so I meditate early in the morning, usually around 5:30 a.m. My energy is highest then. When is your energy highest? Until my heart attack, I meditated after jogging. Now I meditate before I exercise. If you have an exercise practice, see if you find it easier to meditate before your workout or afterwards. It is very personal, just like your 12-Step Program.

How Long to Meditate?

I sit in meditation for forty-five minutes daily. The only exceptions have been times I have participated in silent meditation retreats, when we sometimes sit for one hour.

A good suggestion I was given when I first started meditation practice in 1992 was to begin with a short meditation period and then slowly and gradually increase the duration. I began with ten minutes each day for a week or so, and increased in five-minute increments over the next few weeks to forty-five minutes, where I have stayed ever since.

Be careful not to overdo it, especially at first, because burnout may result. Start with what feels comfortable to you. You may only want to try one minute, three minutes or five minutes at first. That is perfectly fine. Keep in mind two important points:

1. **Decide in Advance.** Decide how long you will sit *before* you sit down, not after you have begun to meditate. Whatever length you choose to sit, *stick to it no matter what.* Make it a serious commitment, just like you have made to your recovery, because it *is* part of your recovery. If you need to do this by starting out sitting one minute or even thirty seconds, fine.

2. **Shorter, Not Longer.** In deciding how long to sit when you begin your meditation practice, I suggest you choose a period that is a bit *shorter* than you think you can easily accomplish. I used this approach when I began meditating. For me, accomplishing what I set out to do and *being ready and willing for more* was much preferable to taking a chance of even slightly overdoing it and then feeling as though it had been *difficult* for me. Meditation is not an endurance contest; no prizes are awarded. Gentleness is indicated. Even if you feel you want to sit *more* than your chosen time, *don't do it.* Get up, walk around for a while, read the paper, brush your teeth, whatever, and *then*, if you still feel the urge to meditate more, sit again.

Timing.

How do you know when your meditation time is up? A woman once told me she just *knows* when her meditation time is over. That's great for her, but it doesn't work for me. For several years, I have used a sports wristwatch with a timer I set to forty-five minutes. When forty-five minutes have passed, it beeps and I know my allotted meditation time has elapsed. If you do not have a stopwatch, you can use a silent digital kitchen or similar timer with an electronic beeper. There are now meditation timer apps you can download to your phone or tablet.

Peeking.

If you are like me, a recurring thought during your meditation practice is, "How much time is left?" Except on silent meditation retreats, I rarely look at my watch during meditation. (I peeked once when it seemed too much time had passed and indeed it had been fifteen minutes past my chosen time; my timer watch had broken.) Why? Because I do not want to get into the habit of distracting myself from my practice; enough desire for distraction already exists. My watch will beep when time is up. As it says in our literature, we do not take the bread out of the oven until it has finished baking; so, too, I do not finish meditating until the beeper sounds.

There is another point about not peeking. When I am meditating and I wonder "How much time is left" or "How long until breakfast" or "I have things to do," those are thoughts that I can use as part of my meditation for deeper looking — for instance, deeply looking at impatience or desire. Or if I am uncertain how much time has passed, I get the chance to sit with and learn to become comfortably familiar with feelings of uncertainty and perhaps mild anxiety. I will explain more about this in Chapter 11 (*Meditating with Feelings*) and Chapter 12 (*Meditating with Thoughts*).

Finding Time.

Many people have told me they would like to have a daily meditation practice, they really would, but they just cannot find the time. My father says there is always time to do the things you want to do. If you are too busy to meditate and work the Program, then maybe you are too busy. Think about that. You might deeply reflect what your priorities are and what they might be. To what length are you willing to go to get what the Program offers?

Try an experiment. When you decide to sit down to meditate and those voices arise trying to talk you out of it, pay close attention to those voices. They are the same ones that are always talking you out of your better judgment.

> Let yourself realize you WANT to practice and then start paying very close attention to the voices that try to talk you out of it.[26]

Fair Weather or Foul.

My physical, mental or emotional state at the time of daily meditation has no bearing whatsoever on decision to sit that day, any more than my decision to meditate that day depends on the weather. If I only sit when I am in the mood to do it or am feeling good, then I am missing the essence of meditation — to observe myself under all conditions, to penetrate the nature of those conditions, and to see how I seek or avoid those conditions. In 1997 I experienced a mild heart attack and emergency angioplasty. I was hospitalized early in the morning, just before I was about to do my daily sitting. In the cath lab I meditated as best I could. Within a couple of hours after they moved me to the coronary intensive care unit, I did my meditation practice for the day (lying down). I practiced each day in the hospital. Part of what the Program teaches is that my circumstances are secondary, but my recovery, my attitude and my actions are primary.

> In all sorts of weather, we steady and deepen our prayer, meditation, and discipline, learning how to see with honesty and compassion, how to let go, how to love more deeply.[27]

So often we know what to do, but instead of doing it we just talk about it. No wonder it does not do us any good.

> A man became sick and went to the doctor for help. The doctor examined him and then wrote a prescription for some medicine. The man returned home and he put up a picture of the doctor on his mantelpiece. Then he bowed to the picture and offered it flowers and incense. And then he took out the prescription and he very solemnly recited it: "Two pills in the morning! Two pills in the afternoon! Two pills in the evening!" All day, all night long he kept reciting the prescription because he had great faith in the doctor, but still the prescription did not help him regain his health.

> The man decided he wanted to know more about the prescription, so he returned to the doctor and asked him, "What is the chemical composition of this medicine? Why did you prescribe it? How does it work?" The doctor explains, "Well, look, this is your disease, and this is the cause of your disease. If you take the medicine I have prescribed, it will eradicate the cause of your disease. When we eradicate the cause, the disease will automatically disappear." The

man thought, "Ah, wonderful! My doctor is so intelligent! His prescriptions are so helpful!" And he went home and started arguing with his friends and neighbors, "My doctor is the best doctor! All the other doctors are useless!"

What does the man gain by such arguments? All his life he may continue fighting and talking about the prescription, but this does not help him at all. If he *takes* the medicine, only then will the man be relieved of his disease. Only then will the medicine help him.[28]

CHAPTER 6

Where to Meditate?

Cat sits in the sun,
Dog sits in the grass.
Turtle sits on the rock.
Frog sits on the lily pad.
Why aren't people so smart?

—Deng Ming-Do

All meditation books and teachers I know of tell you having a regular place to meditate is preferred. I think the value of a regular place is that it conditions through association. On some level I tell myself, "This is the place where I meditate," and somehow the process becomes easier and more inviting.

I do my daily meditation practice in the same place 90% of the time. Occasionally I want variety, so I sit in a particular easy chair in my bedroom. Of course, if I am out of town I make do with whatever is available. Place is important, but it is secondary to the practice; I would not use "inappropriate place" as an excuse to avoid practice.

Location, Location, Location.

I suggest the place where you regularly meditate be as quiet and free from distractions as possible, a place where you can be alone and undisturbed for the entire sitting period. This can be quite a challenge for many people, especially those with families. If you have an extra room you can use solely for meditation (and prayer, if you wish), that is great. Or maybe there is a room in your home that is not used much, like a sewing room or a storage room, where you can arrange a corner to your liking. If none of these is available, perhaps just a favorite easy chair where you can practice your meditation along with other parts of your Program, such as reading the literature or prayer. It is all a matter of personal preference and availability.

The point is that you want the place where you meditate to be warm, inviting and special to you, a wellspring of spirit to create an atmosphere that is conducive to what you are trying to do with your meditation practice — improve conscious contact with your Higher Power.

When I lived alone (with my two dogs) in a three-bedroom house, I was lucky enough to have an entire room set aside exclusively for meditation. Some people would call it a "second bedroom," but I called it the "Meditorium." Just for fun. Now that I am married, I simply find a quiet place in the house for my meditation practice.

Customizing the Meditation Area.

Consider customizing your meditation room or area to make it as conducive as possible to your practice. For some people, placing meaningful objects is helpful, perhaps candles, flowers, religious objects, or photographs of special places or special people. Others may want the room or area to be sparsely furnished. For me, a neat and clean area is best.

In my Meditorium, the only furniture was an old oak chest set against the far wall. Draped over the chest was a cloth covered with Sanskrit writing. About a dozen small objects were atop the chest. The objects were a variety of things that had special meaning to me, a collection of little treasures and curiosities: my recovery birthday chips; a toy ambulance (which reminds me of my unskillful inclination to experience life as an emergency); a bracelet with an inscription which translates roughly as, "I honor the divinity in you"; a fortune-telling 8-ball; a feather, a rock and a pine cone that I found during different meditation retreats; a brass bell; three malas or sets of prayer beads; a postcard from Kansas with a drawing of Dorothy, Toto, the Tin Man, the Cowardly Lion and the Scarecrow, bearing the words, "There's No Place Like Home"; an "I'm Here Now" bumper sticker; and some dried flower petals blessed by a spiritual teacher from India. The objects were not idols or even sacred objects. I did not worship or revere them. I just liked them. To me they were each tangible symbols or reminders of some value or experience.

On the center of the chest was a statue of the Buddha, meditator par excellence. Seated in meditation, quite happy, joyous and free, the statue reminded me of my recovery and the path I had chosen. I did not worship the statue or the Buddha it represents. In fact, over the Buddha's face I taped a photograph of my face taken when I was about nine years old. This whimsically reminded me that the improved conscious contact I seek is within me, not in some external object. It also reminded me not to create idols. Oh, yes, in the Buddha's lap I placed a lapel button bearing the words, "My karma ran over my dogma."

I considered the oak chest to be both an "altar" and an "alter." It is an "altar" in the sense that it was a piece of furniture used in rituals. It was an "alter" in the sense that it was used to help me to "change the things I can."

On my walls in the Meditorium, I have a "Little Buddha" movie poster, a photograph of a young Thai monk holding a book, two colorful Tibetan wall hangings, and above the chest is a framed Japanese print with a poem that translated means, "Pure white birds set against emerald waters. Green mountains ablaze with blooming flowers." The print also bears an *enso*, a calligraphy circle that is a Zen symbol of Enlightenment. Incidentally, I take the term "Enlightenment" to be roughly synonymous with "perfect" conscious contact with my Higher Power.

The only other furnishings in the Meditorium were the cushions on which I meditate. I will discuss these more in Chapter 7 (*Meditation Posture*).

I sometimes burned Japanese incense when I meditated in the Meditorium, perhaps a residue from the '60's. The difference in the 90's was that I was not using the incense to cover up the smell of marijuana, but just because I loved the rich, delicate scent and to watch the smoke arise and pass away.

This room, the Meditorium, was the physical space I created for meditation. I encourage you to do the same. Again, experiment. I have found that as my recovery and meditation practice changed, so, too, did the Meditorium.

What to Wear.

You can wear anything you want when you meditate, but a general suggestion may be helpful — wear loose-fitting, soft clothing, because you do not want to restrict the flow of blood and because they are more comfortable. No thick clothes, no shoes, no belt. Sometimes I sit naked, but only if I'm alone.

It's often difficult to know whether or not to discuss aspects of the Program with your family of origin, but sometimes they surprise you.

> A few days before I left for my first weekend silent meditation retreat years ago, my Dad stopped by my office one afternoon for a fatherly visit. We chatted about various things. After a while he asked me to tell him about the upcoming meditation retreat — where it was to take place, why I was going, what I expected, and so forth. During the conversation Dad asked me how to meditate. I explained briefly how it works.
>
> "That's meditation? I meditate, too," he said.
>
> "You *do*," I said, trying to conceal my amazement. My father? You never know about people.
>
> "Yes, I think I do. At night in bed after I've finished reading, I turn out the light and try to relax before I go to sleep. You know how your mind races sometimes and you just keep thinking and thinking?"
>
> "Sure," I said. Mind-chatter! He's aware of his monkey mind! What's going on here?
>
> He continued, "So I try to watch my breathing, because it helps me relax."
>
> "Yes," I said. Holy smokes. He follows his breath!
>
> "After watching my breathing for a while, I'm pretty relaxed," Dad continued. "But sometimes following my breathing doesn't work and I still can't get to sleep."

"Yes," I said tentatively, thinking, "Uh-oh."

"So then, I get out of bed, drink a large shot or two of scotch, take one of your mother's tranquilizers, get back in bed, and then I go right to sleep. Meditation really works."

CHAPTER 7

Meditation Posture

If form is straight, shadow is straight.

—Taisen Deshimaru

Everyone knows how to sit, but not everyone knows how to sit in order to meditate. Believe it or not, aspects of how to sit to meditate such as how to hold your hands can be contentious among some meditators and reminds me of the two warring factions in *Gulliver's Travels* whose great dispute was over whether to break eggs at the Big End or the Little End. Still proper, or at least adequate, sitting posture is important because it strengthens and shapes meditation.

Meditation Posture.

A good meditation posture will enhance your meditation. Here are a few pointers.

1. **Stability**. You want your body to be a stable platform to support your meditation. If your body is stable, you will be less distracted by it and you can more easily focus on your meditation.

2. **Stillness**. The stillness of your body is reflected by the stillness of your mind. Stilling or calming the mind is one result of meditation.

3. **Strength**. A strong posture allows you to sit for longer periods with less discomfort and sleepiness. Just as recovery requires repeated, consistent effort, there is a certain training aspect to meditation practice.

4. **Reflection**. Meditation posture is "not merely a means, any more than eating, sleeping or hugging your children are means or methods."[29] In a real way, posture reflects our recovery. If we

meditate slouched over, our meditation and recovery will be slouchy. If we are stiff and rigid, our meditation and recovery will be stiff and rigid. If we are erect, supple and fully present, our meditation and recovery will mirror that, too. In this sense, "to take our posture itself is the purpose of [meditation] practice"[30] because it expresses who we are in that very moment of recovery. And who we are in each moment determines who we are becoming in the next moment.

Sitting and Kneeling.

Our Program talks a lot about "hitting your knees," which is a traditional Western posture for approaching a Higher Power. Other cultures and spiritual traditions employ different postures, such as deep bowing and prostrations. Sitting in meditation is the traditional (but not the only) posture for formal meditation. A sitting posture for meditation does not preclude kneeling to pray.

1. **Floor or Chair?** It does not matter if you sit on a chair or on the floor. For more than ten years, I preferred to sit on the floor on a cushion. I tried two other kneeling positions using a *seiza* bench (which is a small sitting bench) and a round pillow upright on edge between my legs to see if I could sit more comfortably for longer periods. If it is more comfortable, then by all means, sit on a chair. I have done so often in the last ten years. Remember that sitting meditation is probably the best foundation for your practice, but you can practice meditation anywhere, anytime or under any circumstances — sitting, standing, lying or walking. When I attend meditation retreats, half my meditation time is spent on a cushion and half the time in a chair.

2. **Cushion.** Use a firm, thick cushion or a folded blanket (at least 6" high) to sit on the floor. The point of using a cushion is not merely comfort. By sitting on the front third of the cushion with your legs crossed in front of you, you will position your pelvis to cause your spine to assume and maintain an erect posture. Although you don't need a special cushion to meditate, several types are available.

I use a Japanese meditation cushion called a *zafu*. Consider placing your cushion on top of another low, flat cushion, a blanket or another padding to protect your legs, shins and ankles. Zafus and a host of other meditation supplies such as incense and bells, can be ordered from suppliers like DharmaCrafts (dharmacrafts.com) or other similar business you can find listed on such magazine websites as *Tricycle* and *Shambhala Sun*.

3. **Seiza Bench.** I sometimes meditate using a seiza bench, which is a little bench (about 7" tall) on which you sit in a kneeling position with your legs folded under you.

4. **Chair.** Sitting in a chair to meditate is perfectly fine, too, but try using one with a firm and level seat and a straight back. Some teachers say there should be no arms on the chair and not to use them if there are. As with the cushion, you should sit toward the front of the chair with your feet flat on the floor, not using the back of the chair for support. For me this manner of using the chair is honored more in the breach than in practice, which is an indirect way of saying I don't follow this suggestion very well when I meditate in a chair.

Legs.

Legs are a problem for some people. Most seated meditation postures have your legs crossed closely in front of you in some fashion. A full-lotus position is preferable but may be difficult or impossible for most Westerners. It is for me. There are other crossed-leg positions, like the half-lotus or Burmese styles. These are illustrated in available meditation books and online.

Spine.

Perhaps the most important thing in your meditation posture is keeping your spine straight. Your spine should be supple and erect, but not rigid or ramrod straight. Sit up straight, being careful not to lean to the right or left, forward or backward.

Head.

Your head should be held up in line with your spine. Tilt you chin very slightly in; gently hold your head as if you are trying to point at the ceiling with the top of your head. Your ears should be in line with your shoulders, your nose in line with your navel, and your shoulders in line with your hips.

Eyes.

You can meditate with your eyes closed or open. You might experiment to see what works best for you, since there are advantages and disadvantages to both. Sitting with eyes closed is most common. It eliminates most (but not all) visual distractions and fosters introspection.

Some people find keeping their eyes closed for an entire meditation period invites sleepiness or dreaminess, so they prefer to sit with eyes open. Eyes "open" can mean anything from eyes completely open to eyes almost closed or anywhere in between. If your eyes are open, I recommend you cast your eyes down at a 45-degree angle about three feet out in front of you. Use "soft eyes," which means not focusing on anything in particular. See without looking. I find a one-third open-eyed position, "looking" at the inside of my eyelids, to be a good method for me. Since my eyes are open a little, I can avoid dreaminess, but I maintain the sense of awareness. If I feel sleepy, I open my eyes completely for a moment or stand up and mediate for a few minutes. Also, since our daily lives are lived eyes open, some suggest that eyes open meditation eases bringing a meditative attitude to daily life "off the cushion."

Mouth.

Close your mouth (good general advice in any event) with your lips together. Hold your teeth and jaws slightly apart. Keep your tongue on the roof of your mouth, with the tip of the tongue comfortably behind the upper teeth at the gum line. Some people don't know what to do if saliva collects in their mouth. This I do know — swallow.

Hands.

You may hold your hands in any of several ways. For the last twenty years, I have usually placed my hands open, palms down on my knees. I do not exert any pressure on my knees, yet I sense a little extra support for my back this way. Most people meditate with their hands together in their lap in some fashion. Perhaps the simplest is holding the thumb of one hand in the lightly closed other hand.

Don't Just Do Something — Sit There.

Try to remain as still as possible; physical movement jars the mind. Physical sensations, feelings, thoughts and mind states (like desire, anger, sleepiness, restlessness, doubt, compassion, equanimity, loving kindness and joy) which arise concerning movement and being still are fodder for your meditation.

A true story, alas, about how to sit and How to Sit correctly!

> I twice attended a yearly event where my ex-wife's spiritual teacher from India makes a public appearance. More than a thousand people attend this colorful occasion, with all manner of people present.
>
> During this event, there are a few periods of meditation. The first year I attended, I noticed a bearded young man who appeared to sit in *extremely* intense meditation for longs periods, even when nobody else meditated. I also noticed he was holding his head "wrong" — bent back at the neck at a 45 degree angle instead of straight on his spine. As one who understood, as few others could, that this man's spiritual life was in my hands, I decided I needed to Fix Him.

As the year's event approached, I decided What To Do. I made a photocopy of two drawings from one of my meditation books. These drawings showed a silhouette of a man in seated meditation, in identical poses except that in one drawing he held his head in Correct Head Position (my way) and in the other his head was in the Incorrect Head Position (his way). It was a perfect illustration of his Error. Though the two drawings were labeled Correct Head Position and Incorrect Head Position, to make Absolutely Certain he did not miss the Error of His Ways, I drew sharp red lines on the copy to emphasize the angle of the Incorrect Head Position so he could not possibly fail to see what he was doing Wrong. My plan was to drop this drawing onto his cushion next to him while he was meditating (discreetly folded; please, I'm not crass) so he would find it when he opened his eyes. My idea was he would open his eyes, see the drawing, achieve Perfect Head Position, appreciate his anonymous Correct Head Position Sponsor, and live happily, joyously and freely ever after.

My dream was not to be. When I arrived at the hotel where the event was being held with my folded Head Position Diagram Truth in my pocket, I was fully prepared to go forward with Plan. Unfortunately, the man failed to comply because he did not attend. This was another example of God doing for me what I could not do for myself — mind my own business.

P.S. If you happen to overhear my next 5ᵗʰ Step, you might also hear that I saved that damned drawing for next year's event!

Chapter 8

Breath and Breathing

Breath is a bridge which connects life to consciousness,
which unites your body to your thoughts.

—Thich Nhat Hanh

Most meditation forms use some concentration technique as a means
to anchor the mind. In the type of meditation I practice, insight
meditation, the breath and breathing are the basic focus of
meditation. It is home base.

Why the breath and breathing? Well, for one thing, the breath is
always there, portable and available, so finding it is easy and
observing it is easy. The heartbeat is also always there, but it is not so
easy to find or observe. The breath connects our bodies to our hearts
and minds, literally and figuratively. Breath resides right at the border
between inner world and the outer world.

We often speak of breath as life itself. Could there be a better
focus for meditation than the ebbing and flowing of life itself?
Something else about the breath and breathing makes it a perfect
focus for meditation. Breathing differs from other bodily
functions because it is both autonomous and volitional. If we
never think about it again, we will continue to breathe without any
conscious effort. Yet we can participate in and exert some
voluntary control over our breathing within certain limits — we
can hold it, speed it up, slow it down, regulate it in various ways.
For me, the breath reflects my relationship with my Higher Power.
Like the breath, even if I am not conscious of my Higher Power it
continues to exist and influence my life. I can choose to be in
conscious contact with my breath or my Higher Power anytime.
Why not now? Learning to be conscious of the breath also teaches

being in the present moment, which is where the breath and breathing occur and where a Higher Power abides.

Each breath can teach the most basic yet subtle principles of the Program. Each breath. For instance, we may have some control over our breath, but ultimately that control is so limited that it is illusory. For instance, eventually we have to exhale, to let the breath go; this is a life-and-death object lesson in letting go, in powerlessness, in faith.

A regular theme of 12-Step recovery grows out of the spiritual challenge inherent in "Thy will, not my will, be done." We learn we are powerless over people, places and situations, as well as certain substances and behaviors, yet we are not helpless. We perceive God as all-powerful, but we are not just supposed to sit there waiting for God to do His will. We must do the footwork. The advice to the shipwreck survivors was, "Pray to God, but row to shore."

For me today, my Higher Power manifests throughout the universe — from galaxies to morning glories, novas to neurons, stars to subatomic particles. What is there that is not of divine nature? I see my Higher Power's presence in the breath and breathing. Inspiration, expiration. One after another. Inhalation, exhalation. Over and over. A continuous process, not an event. If we observe the process of breathing closely, we see it consists of an in-breath, a brief pause, and an out-breath. A beginning, a middle, and an end. Arising and passing away. What else is like that? Everything. What of creation is not like that? Nothing. Every object and every process in the universe has a beginning, a middle, and an end. Everything is in constant change and transformation. This is as true of stars as of stones. With stars and stones, sometimes it is a little hard to discern because of enormous distance, great sweeps of time, or other factors, but change is there. A beginning, a middle, and an end. Observing the breath can be a fascinating learning experience because we can see the universal process in action. And far more wisdom results from direct experience of a Higher Power than it does from mere thinking about a Higher Power. Meditation is that direct experience.

Granted following your breath and breathing may seem boring at first, but if you stick with it for a few weeks you will find it as interesting as this meditation student.

> There is a traditional story about a Zen student who complained to his master that following the breath was boring. The Zen master grabbed the student and held his head under water for quite a long time while the student struggled to come up. When he finally let the student up, gasping for breath, the Zen master asked him whether he had found the breath boring in those moments under water.[31]

CHAPTER 9

Attitude

One sure clue as to whether or not we're being motivated by aspiration or expectation is that aspiration is always satisfying; it may not be pleasant, but it is always satisfying. Expectation, on the other hand, is always unsatisfying, because it comes from our little minds, our egos.

—Charlotte Joko Beck

In our 12-Step Program, we stress changing attitudes as part of "changing the things we can." The Program teaches us the miraculous fact that we *can* change our attitudes; incredibly, the Steps go even further to show us *how* to do it. Perhaps no other recovery tool demonstrates this more directly and immediately than meditation.

But one reality I can create — the point of view I bring to any experience.[32]

The attitude we bring to our 11th Step meditation practice is vital to how much and in what ways we will change, just as the attitude we bring to meetings, doing a 4th Step, going to work and living with our spouse affects them. One thing we do have power over is our perspective — the attitude we bring to any experience. There is a huge difference between "What I experience depends on what happens to me" and "What I experience depends upon how I look at what happens to me." Modern physics recognizes the principle that at some level the very process of observation can change what we observe. What we experience depends on the attitude with which we look.

There is a crucial movement from the idea that "I experience what I experience because things happen to me" to "I experience what I experience because of who I am."[33]

Four Skillful Attitudes.

The attitude we bring to our meditation practice directly shapes the meditation experience. Here are four important attitudes.

1. **No expectations.** As in recovery generally, just doing the footwork of meditation is all that is required. Any more is too much. See what happens, as if we are conducting an experiment. Give it a chance. Abandon any expectations and let our only aspiration be discovery of our own true nature. Don't force or hold onto results. Like everything else in recovery, meditation is a process, not an event. When we have expectations about meditation, when we are trying to "get something" out of it, we are like a fish in water crying out in thirst.

2. **Accept whatever arises and let it go.** During meditation, we will have good (wanted), bad (unwanted) and neutral physical sensations, feelings, thoughts and mind states. Whatever arises, don't grasp them or reject them; just relax and let them arise and pass away. Observe them mindfully by cultivating an attitude of neutral but compassionate acceptance, of letting go, of detachment with love.

3. **Be gentle.** Don't judge the quality of your meditation. We can't do it wrong (though certain techniques may be more effective), so forget such perfectionistic thinking. Progress, not perfection, is key to our meditation practice. Remember we do not meditate to become good meditators; we meditate to improve conscious contact with our Higher Power.

4. **Great Faith, Great Doubt and Great Determination.** It is traditionally said that a skillful meditator will manifest these three attitudes. "Great Faith" is having confidence in meditation as a crucial part of the Steps and that our efforts are maturing in due course. It does not mean blind faith or a suspension of reason. "Great Doubt" is having the willingness, honesty, and openmindedness to look at our most basic life assumptions and opinions with fresh eyes, a "beginner's mind," and an acknowledgment that we do not have all the

answers. It is not knee-jerk skepticism. "Great Determination" is the conscious choice to persevere with all aspects of our Program (including meditation) one day at a time and to let the Program work us, as it will. It is not grim endurance but joyous discovery.

Rituals.

We create and express our attitude in physical actions when we practice meditation. We can call these physical actions "rituals," which *Webster's Third International Dictionary* defines as:

> any practice done or regularly repeated in a set precise manner so as to satisfy one's sense of fitness and often felt to have a symbolic or quasi-symbolic significance.

Some people are put off or even offended by ritual — at least the rituals of others. Think about your very first 12-Step meeting. Remember all the strange rituals you encountered there, from the things repeatedly said ("My name is_____"and the responsive "Hi, ," "You're in the right place," "Keep coming back") to the things repeatedly done (reading the traditional opening, closing and the Steps; passing the basket; reciting the Serenity Prayer and Lord's Prayer; and holding hands in a circle)? Like many of you, I have come to find great comfort and security in the "rituals" of 12-Step meetings; I see them as fostering the miraculous process that occurs there.

The meditation rituals I employ are techniques to adjust my attitude as a part of my meditation practice. For me, my rituals for meditation practice have been as supportive of it (but quite secondary) as creating a physical space where I meditate and for the same reasons. Like my Meditorium, I want the physical acts to be regular, comfortable, and conducive to what I am trying to do — improve my conscious contact with my Higher Power. Rituals can help defeat what my conditioning tells me to do, which often is to blow it off and go eat breakfast. For me to grow spiritually, I must break my unhealthy conditioning. The places where I most need to grow are those places which are most strongly defended and about which I have the greatest denial.

Going through these particular actions is not magic intended to produce a particular result. These rituals are not set in granite. If they ever became fixed, sacred, or even necessary in any way, I would be in deep spiritual danger. They are just fun to do and help get me in the mood, something like what a baseball batter does before he takes a pitch. I don't do these rituals each time I meditate and when I don't my meditation is unaffected. There is nothing of inherent use or value in them to anyone but me. This reminds me of the cautionary Zen story that I will paraphrase this way:

> Once there was a Zen student who for years had sincerely sought Enlightenment. He had followed his Master's instructions to the letter, yet Enlightenment seemed to be as far away as ever. One day while walking in the monastery garden raking leaves, the student accidentally kicked a pebble into a stalk of bamboo. At the sound of the pebble hitting the bamboo, the student achieved the Enlightenment he had sought so long. Eventually he told the other students of his experience. Before very long, the other students were walking all day in the garden, deliberately kicking pebbles into bamboo stalks.

You may decide you do not need any ritual at all, but I suggest you consider what actions bracketing your meditation might better foster this 11th Step meditation work. Again, experiment. See what works for you.

Here are some actions I take before I sit to meditate:

- First, I stand still in front of my meditation cushion. This brings to conscious awareness that meditation transforms me from a human *doing* into a human *being*
- Second, I recite, "I am training to choose what is fundamentally skillful, which is returning awareness to the breath without judgment or gaining idea." This phrase succinctly reminds me:
    - meditation, like working the Steps, is "training" because it requires *practice*, ongoing effort. I see my meditation practice and, indeed, my entire 12-Step Program, as training my thoughts and actions. We cannot get recovery except through our own experience. This is why we practice spiritual work.

➥ I am making choices — to work a 12-Step Program today; to meditate; to live in the Here and Now; and when my mind wanders from the Here and Now, to return awareness to the breath.

➥ being judgmental is one of my primary character defects. Meditation allows me to work with this quality (and others) at the most basic level. For instance, when my mind wanders from my breath to planning the day or having some imaginary conversation, I return awareness to my breath without *judgment*. This is quite different from the judgmental, "Oh, I am out there again in la-la land. I am such a lousy meditator, I'll never get it right, I've been practicing for so many years, so why can't I get it yet?" This is the very kind of self-flagellation that brought me to recovery in the first place. If I cannot learn compassion for myself, how can I have it for others? Only if I can learn compassion for myself, can I have it for others.

➥ there is no "gaining idea." In our 12-Step Program, we talk a lot about doing the footwork, letting go of outcomes, and leaving the results to our Higher Power. We practice this process on a gut level when we meditate. If we cling to the idea that we are going to "get" something out of meditation, we are focused on outcomes, the results and the future. We are trying to "force results," which blocks our way to conscious contact with our Higher Power. In one important sense, there is no improvement in meditation because we are seeking realization rather than attainment. It is only by abandoning any "gaining idea" that we get anything out of it. Another paradox! We are trying to "get" something out of meditation or we wouldn't be practicing it in the first place; yet the only way to "get" it is to give up all expectations.

Meditation is more about "losing" masks, roles, concepts, and opinions in order to discover or recover the reality behind them, like seeing the sun when it finally emerges from behind the clouds after a heavy rainstorm. What we are seeking is the undeluded mind that is eternally present, yet the way to achieve that is by becoming aware of the character defects and conditioning patterns that obstruct that mind.

> So it is not a matter of building up the awakened state of mind [conscious contact], but rather of burning out the confusions which obstruct it.[34]

What we finally come to find underneath when we meditate reminds me of

> the laughter of one who, after searching for something for a long time, suddenly finds it in the pocket of his coat.[35]

When I have concluded my formal daily meditation practice, I usually say these things using traditional phrases meaningful to me:

- First, I remind myself that "life passes quickly and opportunity is lost" and that it is Here and Now I must strive to awaken and improve my conscious contact with my Higher Power.
- Second, I make three mission statements (vows) for the coming day:
  - ➵ to help everyone with their recovery if they ask
  - ➵ to seek my Higher Power everywhere
  - ➵ to ignore emotions which cause inappropriate behavior
- Third, I make five ethical decisions for the coming day:
  - ➵ not to harm others
  - ➵ not to take what is not freely given to me
  - ➵ not to lie or curse
  - ➵ not to engage in substance abuse
  - ➵ not to engage in sexual misconduct
- Fourth, I wish for safety, happiness, health and well-being for myself, my wife, my benefactors, my friends, difficult persons, and all persons everywhere.

My period of formal daily meditation then ends.

In some sense this transitional moment is the most critical in my meditation practice because it is the moment from which the rest of my life proceeds, a new beginning. It is very similar to the end of a 12-Step meeting, when we leave the meeting room and return to our daily lives. If we do not bring what we learned in the meetings to our daily lives, why did we bother going to the meeting in the first place? Likewise, if I do not bring what I experienced during meditation to my daily life off the cushion, why do I bother doing it in the first place?

One attitude that plagues many of us is our need to force results, to get what we want when we want it. Sometimes when we quit seeking to control outcomes and just do the next right thing, the results will be interesting.

> This is a story of a woodcutter and a creature named the Satori. The woodcutter was working in a clearing in the forest, when he looked up and saw a strange animal peeking at him from behind a bush. Thinking to have the animal for dinner, he rushed at it with his ax, but before he could strike, the Satori laughed from the opposite side of the clearing. The creature had the power to read thoughts, and so he knew in advance from where the woodcutter intended to strike. After several attempts, the woodcutter began to grasp the Satori's powers, and naturally thought, "When I see him next, instead of going to where he is, I will go to the opposite side of the clearing." As soon as the woodcutter thought this, though, the Satori appeared at his side and mocked him: "So this is where you think I'm going to be next!" The Satori's taunting continued until the woodcutter became absolutely furious and returned to chopping wood. The Satori laughed and said, "Ah, so you have given up." Just at that moment, as the woodcutter whacked the ax against the tree, its blade flew off and struck the Satori dead.[36]

CHAPTER 10

Meditation Practice

Whatever or whoever arises, train again and again in
looking at it for what it is without calling it names,
without hurling rocks, without averting your eyes. Let
all those stories go. The innermost essence of mind is
without bias. Things arise and things dissolve forever
and ever. That's just the way it works.

—Pema Chödrön

Now let's discuss how to practice the simple meditation style that has
worked for me. I suggest you try because it so seamlessly integrates
with and enhances the Program. Bear in mind there are many other
meditation techniques, so if this one does not appeal to you,
I encourage you to try others. If you look, you will find one.

Finding Your Posture.

Find your posture, sitting or kneeling comfortably with an erect but
supple spine, with your eyes completely or partially closed. Settle in.

Finding Your Breath.

Once your body is settled down and you've found your posture, find
your breath. By this I mean two things. First, notice where you can most
distinctly feel your breathing. Typically this is around the nostril tips or
the upper lip (where you can feel the movement of the breath) or the
chest or the abdomen (where you can feel the movement of the body).
It may take you a while to find this site precisely.

Second, gently focus awareness on the physical process of the in-and-out cycling of the breath at the site you have identified. Try to physically feel or experience (participatorily observe) the actual process of the movement there — the nuances of the felt physical sensations of the "in" and "out" breath at the nose or the rising and falling of the chest or abdomen.

During meditation practice, breathe normally and naturally. Breathe only through your nose, not your mouth. *Do not regulate your breathing in any way.* Meditation is not a breathing exercise. Letting the breath happen naturally as it will is a lesson in relinquishing control, in faith and in letting go that can be applied to our entire lives. Breathe quietly.

Soon you will notice there are many kinds of breath and breathing — fast, slow, shallow, deep, ragged, smooth, strong, light, heavy, soft, etc. You will notice variations in the length of the pause between the in-breath and the out-breath, between the out-breath and the in-breath, and many other subtleties. The more closely you observe, the more you will notice.

Finally, *do not think about or visualize the breath or breathing.* If you do, you will convert a living process into a *concept*, exactly the opposite of what you are trying to do. Simply *experience* the breath and breathing as physical *process*.

Breath Counting.

Breath counting is one method for beginning your meditation practice. (This technique is also used by experienced meditators.) The technique is deceptively simple — silently count your breaths.

Each breath consists of an in-breath and an out-breath. In and out. In and out. In and out. So breathe in, and then as you breathe out, count one. Breathe in, and as you breathe out, count two. Breathe in, and as you breathe out, count three. Continue counting in this way until you complete ten breath cycles. Then start over at one and continue through ten again. Continue counting in this way for the entire period of your meditation.

Now I know this sounds simple, but I can assure you sustaining it for more than a few minutes is difficult for most people at first. Simple, but not easy. Try it.

I still use breath counting, mainly when I realize my mind is unusually distracted.

Following the Breath.

An alternate technique to breath-counting, one preferred by many, is simply to observe or to follow the breath by experiencing physical sensations of the breath and breathing. Instead of counting each breath, simply notice the in-breath and the out-breath as it cycles in and out, in and out. Or you might notice the in-breath, the pause, and the out-breath. You can frame what you experience by silently and gently saying "in" and "out," "arising" and "passing" or other simple words. Like breath-counting, this meditation method is simple, but not easy.

Losing the Breath.

Whether you use breath-counting or breath-following, one of your first discoveries will likely be that you often lose count or lose contact the breath. Suddenly you realize you have no idea what number you are on, that your breath count is way past ten or that you have not followed your breath for a long time. This is perfectly normal. Paradoxically, noticing that you have lost your breath is a gateway to deeper meditation.

Returning to the Breath.

As soon as you become aware you have lost count or lost contact with your breath, gently and without judgment ("I'm not doing this right") return awareness to the breath. If you are breath-counting, start over at one. If you are breath-following, start observing with your next breath. Remembering that everyone loses the breath or count is so important. *Everyone* loses count or loses the breath, over and over and over, but the instruction is always to return awareness to the breath. This is not something we do ten or twenty times; it is something we do thousands and thousands of time. For as long as we meditate.

> Don't suppose you are peculiar because you are forgetful, your mind drifts, and must constantly return to your practice. We are all of us in this together.[37]

As peculiar as it may seem, the process of losing and returning to awareness of the breath is at the heart of meditation practice. Does this sound boring or pointless? If we want to awaken from our sleep, we must do something to learn to bring our attention back to the present moment, to do this more frequently, and to keep our awareness in the present longer.

> For some, this task of coming back [to the breath] a thousand or ten thousand times in meditation may seem boring or even of questionable importance. But how many times have we gone away from the reality of our life? Perhaps a million or ten million times. If we wish to awaken, we have to find our way back here with our full being, our full attention.[38]

The value and wisdom of training ourselves to return to what we are doing in the present moment without judgment is subtle but profound. Even though our minds constantly drift away while meditating, by diligently and relentlessly bringing the focus of our awareness and attention back to the breath, back to the present, we become increasingly able to stay there.

> Even though we constantly slip away in our minds while meditating, losing ourselves for periods of time, we inevitably come back to the observer and thereby increase our skill in distinguishing thoughts as they occur.[39]

I quit meditating when I was in my 20's and again in my 30's precisely because I could not maintain a constant focus on my mantra (a short phrase silently repeated), which I then used rather than the breath. I judged it (and me) a failure because then it meant I was not doing it right, perfectly. So I quit.

Now that I have been in recovery for a while and have studied and, much more importantly, I have practiced meditation on a daily basis, I know that losing count or losing the breath inevitably will occur as long as I meditate. Why? Because losing attention is an inherent part of meditation. Just like making mistakes is an inherent part of being human. Doing even simple meditation techniques perfectly is just not possible, if by perfectly you mean that your mind never wanders from the breath. If you could do *anything* perfectly, you would not need to be in recovery.

The mind has an extremely powerful tendency to become unconcentrated, to wander or drift off into thinking — remembering, planning, worrying or fantasizing, for instance. If you have ever meditated for more than just a few minutes, you have experienced this. A regular meditation practice can reduce the frequency and duration of the wandering mind by training your ability to concentrate the mind, but it cannot eliminate it entirely any more than we can entirely eliminate all our character defects.

It is absolutely critical to the development of a meditation practice for you to experience and understand that the mind's tendency to wander and drift off is *not* a failure. Appreciating and using this tendency presents a subtle but golden opportunity (dozens of times during each meditation session) for tremendous spiritual growth simply by returning awareness to breath-counting or breath-following each time you notice your mind has drifted away. Why? It is practice returning to the present-moment, where we find conscious contact with our Higher Power. Just drop your wandering thinking, let it go and return to the breath. Again, simple, but not easy. Try it.

Labeling.

"Labeling" is another technique. Silently, softly and gently label, note or name what you are experiencing (other than the breath and breathing) that intrudes into and dominates your field of awareness while you are meditating — typically, a physical sensation, a feeling, a thought, a mind state — as soon as you become aware of it. Examples of labels are "thinking," "feeling," "hunger," "planning" and "pain."

Labeling is a technique you can use to strengthen and refine your meditation practice. It answers the question, "What do I do when my mind wanders from my breath and breathing?" In one sense, labeling is an abbreviated way of informing yourself, "My mind has wandered to thinking (or to a physical sensation, a feeling or a mind state) and I now choose to return to my breath and breathing." Although your primary focus of awareness is the breath and breathing, as you meditate your mind will experience mind/body processes other than the breath and breathing. Labeling is framing an experience so that it stands out more clearly and thereby becomes easier to drop.

We can categorize these other mind/body processes generally as follows:

- physical sensations (the breath is only one of many)

- feelings

- thoughts

- mind states (like desire, anger, sleepiness, restlessness, doubt, compassion, equanimity, and joy)

One effect of labeling is to cut off intrusive experiences, which thereby eases the return of awareness to the breath and breathing. Labeling also highlights, on a sensation-by-sensation, feeling-by-feeling, thought-by-thought or mind state-by-mind state basis, where your mind drifts off to and how your mind works, giving you unprecedented and unparalleled access and insight into your mind and how it works.

For instance, if you become aware your neighbor's dog is barking, labeling means to silently note "hearing, hearing." If your neck hurts or you are grieving over your mother's death, note "feeling, feeling." If you are thinking about today's big conference, note "thinking, thinking." You might find it more helpful to be a little more specific than just "thinking, thinking" or "feeling, feeling," such as by silently labeling "planning, planning" or "pain, pain," but getting too specific can lead to conceptualization.

> That label, "thinking," is the beginning of acknowledging that the whole drama doesn't have any substance, that it arises out of nowhere, but it seems extremely vivid.[40]

Process vs. Content.

The labeling technique shifts awareness from the *content* of experience (a barking dog, a painful neck, or what may happen at the upcoming business meeting) to the *process* of that experience (hearing, feeling, thinking, etc.). During meditation we want to ignore the *content* of our thinking and the other intrusive experiences and focus instead on their *process*. As our meditation practice matures, we gradually shift from the level of concept to the level of direct experience. This is an essential part of meditation practice. Use passive words in the labeling technique if possible, like "hearing" rather than "listening" or "seeing" rather than "looking." The labeling technique transforms being caught inside the content of a thought or experience into observing it and its process. Here arises the "wisdom to know the difference." When we label our thinking, we cease squirrel-caging and instead we train in just accepting the feeling, the thought or the mind state for what it is, in just being in the Here and Now, without zoning out. We separate out reactions from the events themselves.

> Pay precise attention, moment by moment, to exactly what you are experiencing right now, separate out your reactions from the raw sensory data.[41]

Focusing on process and not content carries over into our daily lives. As we practice and train our minds, we experience the nature and process of sensations, feelings, thoughts and mind states, instead of identifying with their content. The ability to discern process amid the storm of content is vital to recovery. If I keep my attention on the content of a situation ("She never called me back!"), I will stay in the problem. When I start looking at the process ("I am experiencing anger or hurt, look how these feelings manifest, change and disappear"), I am in the solution. We are trying to awaken from the illusion that the concepts are the reality. A life fully experienced is far richer than a life merely thought about.

> We then take these concepts to be actually existing things and begin to live in the world of concepts, losing sight of the underlying, insubstantial nature of phenomena . . . Our practice is to awaken from the illusion of taking concepts to be the reality, so that we can live in clear awareness of how things actually are.[42]

A Word of Caution.

Whatever meditation technique you decide to use, a word of caution. Meditation is like a raft used to get across a river to the other shore. When you land on the other shore, you abandon the raft because you don't need it anymore; you don't carry it around once you've landed.

Likewise, meditation is a means to an end, not an end in itself. Becoming too attached to your technique, treating it like a Higher Power, is a pitfall to avoid.

Farming is like meditation; if you do not go out into the fields and work, you will not have much of a crop.

> The young salesman approached the farmer and began to talk excitedly about the book he was carrying. "This book will tell you everything you need to know about farming," the young man said enthusiastically. "It tells you when to sow and when to reap. It tells you about weather, what to expect and when to expect it. This book tells you all you need to know."
>
> "Young man," the farmer said, "that's not my problem. I know everything that is in that book. My problem is doing it."[43]

CHAPTER 11

Meditating with Feelings

. . . [T]ry giving up your habitual patterns. It leaves
you with the same kind of queasy feeling that you
have when giving up any other addiction.

—Pema Chödrön

When we begin meditating, we immediately observe the five senses
(seeing, hearing, tasting, smelling and touch) and emotions continue
unabated during our practice. Sensations and emotions arise and pass
away while we meditate. How could it be otherwise? But we do not
meditate *in order* to see, hear, taste, smell, touch or have emotions. We
experience sensations and emotions during meditation, but we do not
directly heed them. How can we skillfully handle the two chief types
of feelings — physical sensations and emotions — in meditation?

Feelings.

1. **Physical Sensations.** Besides the sensations of the breath
    and breathing, our mind perceives myriad other physical
    body sensations — tingling, aching, itching, throbbing,
    coolness, warmth, softness, hardness, all the normal everyday
    sensations, along with various sights, sounds, smells and tastes.
    Perhaps we tend to notice these physical sensations more
    when we are meditating because we are so quiet and still. It
    is important to be aware not so much of the sensations
    themselves, but how they constantly change and how they arise
    and pass away.

2. **Emotions.** As with the physical sensations, because we are
    quiet and still, we generally tend to notice the emotions

more distinctly. As with sensations (and everything else we experience during meditation), what is important to be aware of is not so much our emotions themselves, but how they constantly change, how they arise and pass away.

Many of us in recovery have had considerable difficulties with our emotions. These difficulties have two common aspects. First, some of us have trouble recognizing, acknowledging and appropriately expressing them. Perhaps this comes from years of stuffing them — denying, minimizing, suppressing, repressing — to avoid what we perceive as the unpleasant consequences (internal, external or both) of doing so. Second, for some of us our emotions can seem so overwhelming that they seem to threaten us or others.

> These mental states are troublesome mainly because
> we tend to identify with them.[44]

A powerful benefit of meditation for me has been a marked improvement in my ability to handle my emotions, to experience, acknowledge, express and communicate them, and to learn to be comfortable with even the most unpleasant ones. This is because in meditation I have become intimately more familiar with them.

Conditioning.

The feelings — physical sensations and emotions — that we experience and how we think about and act on them result primarily from our conditioning. That conditioning is the same as the conditioning of Pavlov's dogs, who salivated when the bell rang whether or not there was food. Our conditioning is usually far more complex and subtle than a ringing bell, but it is conditioning nonetheless. We have been conditioned mainly by our family, schools, governments, religions, and popular culture, as well as by our own actions and experiences. Conditioning continues throughout our lives, even to the moment of death. We can perceive our 12-Step Program as a method of both *deconditioning* and *reconditioning*, which are methods of changing the things we can. To recover is to awaken from our conditioned sleep of not seeing the truth. To recover is to return to shore from our "drift through the surge of habitual impulses."[45]

Determining the source and nature of our conditioning has value, at least up to a point. Beyond this point, however, knowing its exact source and nature only allows us to be "well-informed prisoners." The constant refrain in recovery is, "Yes, but what can we *do* about it?" One significant effect of meditation is that it allows us to act in an appropriate and skillful way even when it is contrary to our unhealthy conditioning.

Meditating with Feelings.

Meditation allows an opportunity to work with our feelings (sensations and emotions) in a direct manner and at a depth available in no other way. Working in meditation with feelings that are unhealthy conditioned responses erodes or even eliminates them and their power over our future. Once you have experienced a conditioned response with your heart and mind completely open, the result is instant deconditioning and freedom.

Besides dealing with our existing conditioned responses that tend to lead us around by the nose, meditation is also a way to lessen or avoid being further conditioned by them. If we can feel things fully and mindfully, they will not condition the mind.

To illustrate this, suppose you are going to pick me up at 7 p.m. for a movie and you are "late again." Suppose I become angry because "this is the 100th time you have done this to me." Before I found recovery, if you were late again my conditioning would have meant I would shut down emotionally, gripe at you, call you names, cancel our plans, or perhaps behave in a more sideways (indirect) manner such as sarcasm, passive-aggressive behavior or holding a resentment against you.

Recovery gives us a set of multipurpose tools to deal with this and every other situation. Let's compare how two of these Program tools — the Serenity Prayer and meditation — work with my anger that you are "late again".

The Serenity Prayer provides a process to acknowledge and transform my anger or at least my relationship to and perspective of it. It operates primarily, but not exclusively, at a conscious level:

- I ask for the "serenity to accept the things I cannot change," those things over which I am powerless. It is clear from your behavior the other 99 times that you *are* always late. Apparently that is just who you are and the way you behave. What I have learned from the Program is that I am powerless to change you *and* it is not my business to do so even if I could. Thus logically, at least, I can somewhat serenely accept that you are a person who is late and I cannot change you.

- I ask for "courage to change the things I can." In 12-Step recovery I began to understand there is only one thing I *can* change and that one thing goes by the name "me." Now I have several choices — tell you what I want from you (for you to be on time) and then notice whether or not I get it; accept the fact that you are late and let it go; stop making plans with you; and/or make alternative plans in case you do not show upon time (Plan B).

- I ask for "wisdom to know the difference" between what I cannot change (you) and what I can change (me). In this example, the distinction between the two is evident.

Meditation offers a different approach to my anger that you are "late again". It can easily be used along with (but not at the same time) the Serenity Prayer or other recovery tools; it is complementary to all other recovery tools.

How would I work with my feelings (physical sensations and emotions) that "you are late again?" (Of course, there are angry thoughts associated with "you being late," thoughts with which I could meditate. I'll discuss this in the next chapter, Chapter 12 *Meditating with Thoughts.*)

When would I use meditation in these circumstances? Either immediately, when the angry feelings first arise or during my next meditation period.

The practice would be to focus my awareness and mindfulness on the angry feelings rather than the breath and breathing. This is how. I would begin meditation in the usual way, counting or following the breath to stabilize and concentrate my mind. Soon the angry feelings would intrude into my awareness. I would then begin to observe, investigate and penetrate the actual physical sensations associated with the anger. I would closely observe the process (*not* the content) of my anger. Where and how do I physically experience anger? As increased pulse? As a hot flush? As a contraction or tension in my chest, shoulders or neck? As adrenaline? Where? What does it physically feel like? How do these physical sensations arise and pass away? How do they change? I would explore these feelings in minute detail, each nook and cranny of my body where I can feel them. What *are* those feelings, exactly? One insight would inevitably be that the angry feelings are not a solid, undifferentiated mass, but kaleidoscope of various subtle, pulsating sensations which together I call "anger." We become more aware of these experiences as they arise, so we can reduce their power to overwhelm us.

> One of the major benefits of meditation and retreats is that we become more sensitized to these experiences as they arise and are therefore able to minimize the degree to which they overwhelm us.[46]

Seeing Through Feelings.

After working with anger (or any other feelings) for a time in this way, a transformation occurs. The angry feelings (and associated thoughts) diminish or evaporate. This works in three ways:

1. **Deconditioning.** By meditating with feelings, they are no longer directly linked to you being "late again." I simply experience anger and how it feels in my body. This is how the conditioning (stimulus: you are "late again"; response: "I am angry") breaks down and reactivity diminishes. Meditation allows me to break the "you–are–late-again-so–I–am–angry" circuit. I am no longer an angry person who is stuck in the middle of my anger. Instead, I am a person who is experiencing how anger physically feels.

2. **Disidentification.** Very often feelings are so powerful that they overwhelm our sense of who we are. Confusion exists between where we stop and our feelings start. Feelings are troublesome only to the extent that we overly identify with them as "ours." By meditatively watching our feelings arise and pass away, feeling after feeling, one after another, day after day, week after week, month after month, year after year, eventually we cease overly identifying with them. This is disidentification. We become like a mountain peak,

which is unaffected by clouds of feeling which float past in unending succession. Meditation teaches us that feelings are something we have, not who we are.

3.   **Discharge.** All feelings have physical and mental energy associated with them. We experience this very clearly during meditation. The energy in unwanted (rejected) feelings is re-charged with the energy we use to push them away, thus magnifying them. The energy in wanted (grasped) feelings is re-charged with the energy we use to grasp them, thus magnifying them. The energy in feelings neither rejected nor grasped (accepted feelings) simply dissipates by a process of entropy (the natural tendency of energy to degrade and wind down), thus dissipating the feelings. In this way, the feelings are processed and their energy is discharged.

By meditating with anger or other feelings, we come to see them for what they really are. We understand at an experiential level, not intellectual, that the anger or other feelings are specific changing bodily sensations that arise and pass away, just like the breath, one after the other. The feelings are essentially fluid and impermanent, with no fixed reality that deserves, seeks or requires our continuing attention. They are just part of the ever-changing experience of being.

In meditating with anger or other feelings, therefore, we no longer are so attached to them. They are not ours; *they just are.* This insight allows us to accept those feelings, to let them go. Stated differently, we don't let the feelings go as much as they just pass away like a puff of smoke. We might think of this process as the "change the things I can" part of the Serenity Prayer.

We also deeply experience the insight that there is no *fundamental* difference among any of our feelings. It is only our thoughts (*interpretation of, identification with* or *attachment to*) about them that influence our actions in ways that are counter to our own best interests. If we do not interpret, identify with or attach to the feelings, we can actually choose which feelings merit our attention and action and which ones do not. Conscious contact enables conscious conduct.

> Conditioned responses stand between us and direct experience of the world. If we want to be fully present to what is actually going on, we cannot

remain blind to our conditioning. We must see it for what it is and move on into the freedom that lies beyond it. Some courage may be required, because if we step outside the conditioned sense of self and ask, Who am I? There is no answer. That sounds scary. But the good news is that once we go beyond our conditioning, the question of who I am never arises. What fills the gap where my identity used to be is simply experience itself.[47]

I want to emphasize the purpose and effect of meditating with feelings and seeing through them is *not* to make unwanted feelings just go away or to avoid them. That is exactly what brought many of us to our knees and to the doors of recovery in the first place. On the contrary, the purpose and effect of meditating with feelings and seeing through them is to feel and confront these feelings intimately and directly, head and heart on, to observe and feel them precisely, with all our focused attention, and to see what they really are, instead of distracting ourselves from them as we normally do. The only way out is though.

> When the attention is trained on the emotion in question — in particular, on the bodily experience of the emotion — it gradually ceases to be experienced as a static and threatening entity and becomes, instead, a *process* that is defined by time as well as space.[48]

When we encounter unwanted feelings, instead of acting out or repressing them, perhaps we can use the situation as an opportunity to feel our heart. Under all our feelings we will find what it is we are trying to recover.

Meditation is a laboratory for working with feelings; "out there" is where it counts.

Shortly after I entered recovery, I joined a book club in which I only knew a couple of other members. The night of the first meeting I drove over to the home of the book club host. I circled the block several times instead of parking in front of the house, nervous about going in. I had just enough recovery to admit to myself that I was avoiding going into the meeting because of feelings of low self-esteem and anxiety. Just as I was about to turn the car around and return home, I pulled over to the side of the road and stopped the car. I decided to sit with my feelings, as I had been doing in meditation. After a few minutes of experiencing the feelings in my body, I "saw through" them enough to recognize they were just fluid and passing feelings. With this insight, I started the car, drove back over to the book club, and attended the meeting. The feelings no longer controlled my behavior. The only way out was through.

CHAPTER 12

Meditating with Thoughts

The more you talk and think about it,
the further astray you wander from the truth.
Stop talking and thinking,
and there is nothing you will not be able to know.

—Hsin Hsin Ming

To understand meditation better, you might consider the mind as a "sixth" sense organ which thinks. That's just what it does. Like the five ordinary senses, thinking continues during meditation, but we do not meditate *in order to* think.

Meditation calms the mind, which means that it reduces the frequency and duration of thoughts. Meditation does not stop thoughts. My experience has been that no matter what happens, the mind thinks thoughts just as inevitably as the ears hear sounds or the nose smells odors. We do not meditate

to try to get rid of thoughts, but rather to see their true nature. Thoughts run us around in circles if we buy into them, but really they are like dream images. They are like an illusion — not really all that solid.[49]

My Mind Is Out To Get Me.

When we start to practice meditation, we immediately become aware of our thoughts — not only their content, but their incredible number and proliferation. We may be surprised to discover the incessant cascade of thoughts, ideas, monologues, debates, stories, hopes, fears, opinions, beliefs, plans, expectations, memories, regrets, fantasies, and judgments. Realization of the number and proliferation of our thoughts may at first be disturbing or even shocking. We knew vaguely that we thought a lot, but this much? Our thoughts are out of control! All this mind-chatter. And we live with this? One Asian spiritual tradition calls this phenomenon the "monkey mind."

We realize we are powerless over which thoughts arise in our minds. We don't even know where they originate, and we don't know where they go.

But consider — this realization may be our first meditation insight. Our meditation efforts have already paid off. We have become more deeply aware of the existence of our monkey mind, something about which we were previously completely or partially unaware. Awareness is the prerequisite to recovery. Insight into the nature of our thoughts is critical because it plays such a paramount role in our lives.

This incessant mind-chatter subtly distracts us from being fully present, available and open to our experiences, our loved ones, our friends and our Higher Power. How can we be fully present if parts of our minds are off somewhere in the future, the past or some fantasy, chattering away, even if we are not consciously aware of it? If our goal is to improve conscious contact with our Higher Power, somehow we must contend skillfully with this ceaseless mind static and its resultant distraction, which blocks us from the conscious contact we seek. This is exactly what meditation does. But it requires effort.

Most of us are comfortable when we are thinking and uncomfortable when we try to ignore thoughts as they arise. A story line goes on in our minds nearly all the time – "The Story of Me". At first you may deny this is true, but think about it. Stop. Close your eyes for three minutes. Observe what your mind thinks. Maybe you are thinking something like

> Well, this is ridiculous. No story line going on in my mind. This guy's nuts. He reminds me of my Uncle Leo. What a character he is. Oh, I still need to get him a birthday present. Maybe Leo would like a nice tie. I hope he likes it. Where can I get him a tie? How much should I spend? My finances are low right now, so maybe I should just get Uncle Leo a card.

This kind of thinking is constant, though largely unnoticed due to its very constancy. Meditation brings this thinking into the healing light of awareness. Only when we become aware do we have any hope of making changes in our lives.

When we say in the Program that "our best thinking got us here," what we mean is that by relying solely on our own monkey mind and self-will, we became powerless, with unmanageable lives. But for me today, my best thinking (when the monkey is somewhat tamed) *keeps* me working a Program of recovery because I no longer rely solely on my own monkey mind or my own will.

> If we do not come to understand the error in the way
> we think, our self-awareness, which is our greatest
> blessing, is also our downfall.[50]

Thinking and reasoning are crowning aspects of humanity; they have a critical place in our lives, culture and civilization. Nevertheless, constant random thinking prevents deep calmness of our mind and impedes conscious contact with our Higher Power.

> The spring flowers, the autumn moon
> Summer breeze, winter snow.
> If useless things do not clutter your mind
> You have the best days of your life.[51]

Meditation calms the mind, which means it reduces the frequency and intensity of thoughts. When you first begin meditating, your thoughts flow past like water flowing over Niagara Falls. Gradually, as you meditation improves, your thoughts become a gentle mountain stream. Finally, when you are really practiced at it, your thoughts are like a placid mountain lake, with only the occasional ripple marring the surface.

But please be clear on this point — meditation does not stop thoughts. My experience has been that no matter what happens, the mind thinks thoughts just as the ears hear sounds or the nose smells odors. Besides, we do not meditate to make our thoughts go away. We meditate to see their true nature, which is dreamlike, an illusion.

Thoughts vs. Thinking.

When we meditate, we do not engage with our thoughts. By this I mean we do not follow our thoughts, we do not participate in them, and we do not identify with them, all of which would be absorbing ourselves in associative or discursive thinking, not meditation.

Let me give you an example. During meditation, suppose the following thought arises:

> I wonder if my sponsor will be at the noon meeting today?

There. That is a thought. If we simply label it ("thinking, thinking"), let it go and gently return awareness to the breath, we are meditating. Suppose instead it happens this way:

> I wonder if my sponsor will be at the noon meeting today? I haven't seen him lately. I really ought to phone him. I'd like to tell him what Jill said to me. I am so mad at her. She was out of line telling me I am inconsiderate. Who asked her to take my inventory, anyway? I was *not* inconsiderate. I had to stop for gas for my truck. It uses so much gas. I wish gas pumps all had air hoses; my tires were so low. I wonder if I need new tires? But they're expensive. I sure hope Tony pays me that $500 today. I could use the money. Then I could get new tires or maybe that new printer for my computer. I really want a color laser printer. But do I need one? What would I do with it? Oh, I have an idea. I could start that business with Jill. . .

This is not meditating; this is thinking. There is nothing wrong with thinking, mind you, but it is not meditating. The difference in these two scenarios is that in the second one, I *engaged in, participated in and identified with* the first thought, spinning out a story line. A story line is not "wrong," but we do not meditate to create or observe stories. The only insight we get from story lines is the realization that our minds create them constantly, even when we are not aware of it, and that they impede us from conscious contact with our Higher Power.

Temptation and Seduction.

Our thinking has an incredibly powerful enchanting quality. Quite often I have experienced the seductive temptation to engage in associative or discursive thinking rather than meditation.

It is normal during meditation for our mind to wander or drift off from the breath into a story line (a love story, revenge fantasy, re-enactment of an event from yesterday, speculation about what might happen tomorrow at the big meeting, whatever). When we realize this, the meditation instructions are this: gently and without judgment return awareness to the breath and breathing. But it is astounding how tenaciously we sometimes resist returning awareness to the breath because *we want to see what happens in the story.* We think, "Well, wait, I'll return attention to the breath when this story or line of thinking is over." This has happened to me countless times. The mind story is so compelling that I want to see what happens, even though *I am imagining the whole thing as I go!*

Thinking tempts the meditator like the Sirens' song tempted Ulysses. Ulysses was warned the Sirens would charm him as he sailed past their island on his way home. The Sirens' song was so enchantingly sweet, promising wisdom and knowledge of everything that would happen, that everyone who had ever sailed near the island jumped into the deadly sea to reach the Sirens, drowning in the attempt. The Sirens' song was a powerful pull to sailors, just as the temptation to engage in associative or discursive thinking while meditating is to us.

To prevent succumbing to temptation, Ulysses had his men (who had placed thick wax in their own ears) bind him to the mast of his ship so he could not break away to follow the Sirens' song. Thus it was that when the Sirens began to sing, tempting Ulysses to jump into the sea and go to them, he avoided acting on the temptation because he was bound to the mast of his ship. Tying Ulysses to the mast overcame his self-will, which was out of control.

During meditation (and off the cushion), our thoughts can be like the Sirens' song, tempting us to follow them, to spin out stories, plans, ideas, wishes, fantasies, musings when it is unhelpful, distracting or even destructive to do so. The temptation is extremely pernicious. If we bind ourselves to the mast of our breathing, two benefits accrue. First, by resisting the temptation like Ulysses, we can continue our journey. Second, each time we tear ourselves away from discursive thinking, we strengthen our minds, just like doing reps with weights at the gym. This tempting pull is the ego, "my will," not "Thy Will." We can consciously choose not to follow the thought once we become aware of it. Meditation creates that awareness and strengthens our better judgment.

Cultivating the ability to avoid the Sirens' song of discursive thinking helps our recovery. When obsessive thinking, desires or thoughts tempt us during our daily lives, we can better resist them precisely because in meditation we have intimately examined the temptation process, sensations, feelings, thoughts and mind states, and we have practiced letting them all go, hundreds or thousands of times. This is training the mind.

Seeing Through Thoughts.

Perception of the nature of our own thoughts changes subtly but powerfully after we have meditated for a while. As the mind-chatter begins to subside during meditation and there are fewer thoughts, each remaining thought stands out in stark relief against the bright background of the mind's spacious vastness. Most of our thoughts are a consequence of our previous conditioning. Awareness of this reduces our tendency to identify with our thoughts.

> Most of our thoughts are a function of mechanical conditioning and automatic response. This insight works slowly to diminish our tendency to identify with our thoughts.[52]

Then we notice two things. First, we notice that each thought arises and passes away, just like our breath, one after the other without cessation. They are essentially fluid and impermanent. Second, we understand there is *no fundamental* difference among any of our thoughts. It is our *interpretation of, identification with* or *attachment to* these thoughts that causes us to imbue them with a power that governs our behavior. If we do not interpret, identify with or attach to thoughts, we see they are alike in an absolute sense. When that insight occurs, we can choose which thoughts deserve our attention and intention and which ones do not. Conscious contact enables conscious conduct.

We see that the deep calm of meditation is not somewhere else, far away, but right there in front of us, our true nature, under our thoughts.

> The stillness of meditation lies beneath the chattering of the thinking mind, not beyond and separate from it.[53]

Some of us tend to intellectualize everything. I am such an unfortunate whose desire to understand and know often prevents me from working my Program.

> A Newcomer approached an Oldtimer and wanted to have all his philosophical questions about the Program answered before he would work the Steps.

> The Oldtimer said, "You remind me of the man who was seriously hurt in a hit-and-run auto accident. When the paramedics arrived at the scene, the injured man said, 'I won't let you care for me until you tell me about your education, training and experience. The victim died before he received any help."[54]

CHAPTER 13

Opinions and Objectivity

Do not search for the truth;
only cease to cherish opinions.

—Hsin Hsin Ming

We all have opinions, beliefs and ideas about a wide variety of subjects. This is perfectly fine, of course, but being overly attached to our opinions can inhibit our recovery. It can prevent us from experiencing the world as it is and can lead to harm, especially when the opinions become negative judgments upon which we act to the detriment of ourselves and others. Being overly attached to our opinions is being unteachable. So often we come to believe what we think *just because we think it*, even where our opinions are completely contradicted by logic and our own experience.

> The foolish reject what they see,
> not what they think.
> The wise reject what they think,
> not what they see.[55]

For instance, it may be my opinion that the alcoholic in my life should stop drinking. But if I am so attached to that opinion that I act on it by trying to convince, nag or manipulate her into stopping, I am on shaky ground, I am not minding my own business, I am playing God, and we both suffer.

> We have definite opinions about the way things are and should be. This is projection: we project our version of things onto what is there. Thus we become

completely immersed in a world of our own creation,
a world of conflicting values and opinions.[56]

We have definite opinions about the way things are and the way things should be. But then we imagine that our opinions are Truth.

Most people have strong opinions about their form of religion or government, to name two examples. Whether or not they have recently or ever seriously examined those opinions, some people so identify with their opinions that they are willing to judge, persecute or even kill others to propagate them. The Crusades, the Spanish Inquisition, slavery, the Holocaust, and the 2001 Twin Towers destruction are but examples.

Meditation practice enables us to see through our opinions for what they are — changing, transient and essentially insubstantial thoughts that can impede or degrade conscious contact with our Higher Power if we become overly attached to them.

Holding an idea of something is resistance, because
even an idea of what is, is not what is.[57]

Our opinions are only a concept of what is. We must remember that a concept of what is, is not what really is.

Meditation has taught me to try diligently to notice my opinions (whether or not I act on them) as they arise and as they pass away. Many strong opinions I formerly held I now consider "wrong." Admitting this forces me to acknowledge that my opinions will undoubtedly continue to change throughout the rest of my life. How can I tenaciously hold to an opinion I know I may abandon? They are just opinions — not right, not wrong, not fundamentally different from thoughts in their essential fluidity and impermanence. Meditators are generally less prone to believe their own opinions in a way that produces harm. Meditation fosters the ability to see through my opinions. From the famous *Hsin Hsin Ming*, the first Zen poem:

If you wish to see the truth,
then hold no opinions for or against anything.
To set up what you like against what you dislike
Is the disease of the mind.[58]

If someone suggests I might enjoy watching the birds, a sunset or some tulips, I might say, "Why? I already know what they look like. I've seen plenty of them." My pre-existing, frozen opinions of "birds," "sunsets" and "tulips" prevent me from enjoying them as they are now rather than what I "think" they are. Many of us make idols out of our concepts, for which we are willing to act in a harmful manner to protect them.

> Concepts create idols; only wonder comprehends anything. People kill one another over idols. Wonder makes us fall to our knees.[59]

Beginner's Mind.

Meditation teaches seeing the world as a child, so joy returns in the wonder and awe of a world alive and ablaze. The Japanese word, *shoshin*, expresses this "beginner's mind."

> In the beginner's mind there are many possibilities; in the expert's mind there are few.[60]

We develop (recover) beginner's mind by meditation because it allows us to see through some of our frozen opinions and thereby *detach* from, or at least loosen our grip on, them. We resume beginner's mind as our meditation practice deepens, and with that comes the joy and delight of seeing life afresh each day and each moment. This is true freedom.

Objectivity.

> *Objective* — dealing with facts or conditions as perceived without personal opinions, preferences or interpretations.

> *Subjective* — dealing with facts or conditions as perceived conditioned or shaped by personal opinions, preferences or interpretations.

A benefit of a regular meditation practice is increased objectivity. I don't contend that objectivity is necessarily "good" and subjectivity is necessarily "bad." After all, our personal opinions, preferences and interpretations help define who we are. They enrich our experience of life and the joy of living. Still, for those of us who come into recovery suffering and in distress, we discern that it is often our own subjective personal opinions, preferences and interpretations that prevent us from being happy, joyous and free and which impede conscious contact with our Higher Power. Perhaps we cannot change our circumstances, but we can always change our attitude toward our circumstances. Meditation helps us do exactly that.

Each of us views people, places and situations through our own subjective filtering lenses that have three primary settings — good, bad and neutral. We can label these lenses in other ways, such as wanted, unwanted and neutral or pleasant, unpleasant and neutral, for instance, but the point is the same. If we subjectively consider something *good, wanted* or *pleasant*, we desire it, we seek it, we grasp it. If we subjectively consider something *bad, unwanted* or *unpleasant*, we push it away, we avoid it, we reject it. If we subjectively consider something *neutral*, we don't pay much attention to it, we ignore it, we let it alone.

We attach to, identify with and define ourselves by what we consider good, wanted or pleasant. "This is my beautiful new wife; this is my cool new car; I am from California; I am a heart surgeon; I exercise every day; I like jazz recorded on vinyl; this feels so good." Ironically we also attach to, identify with and define ourselves by what we consider bad or unwanted. "My wife nags me constantly; I hate this crummy car; California is so dangerous; my job is too stressful; I am so lazy; I am tired of jazz; I hate this feeling." There being no inherent fixed value in any of these things, our view of them all depends on our attitude toward them.

How do we think and act with respect to something we consider good, wanted or pleasant? We concentrate and focus our self-will, thoughts and actions on getting it, having it, owning it, making it ours, attempting to freeze time and space and to control and manipulate people and situations to keep and hold on to it. The expression, "Alcoholics don't have relationships; they take hostages" comes to mind here for all of us. If we want something enough, we will go to "any length" to get it, sometimes acting outside our own value system to take it, have it, and make it our hostage — no matter what the consequences. Suffering arises because when trying to grasp tightly onto it, we strangle it and simultaneously we give away some of our freedom to it.

How do we think and act with respect to something we consider bad, unwanted or unpleasant? We concentrate and focus our self-will, thoughts and actions on avoiding it, not having it, rejecting it, making it go away, attempting to freeze time and space and to control and manipulate people and situations to keep it away. If we do not want something intensely enough, we will go to "any length" to avoid it, sometimes acting outside our own value system to defeat, reject it, keep it away — and no matter what the consequences. Suffering arises because when trying to push it away, we give it life and we give away some of our freedom to it.

What happens to us when we are constantly labeling things as good, wanted, pleasant or bad, unwanted or unpleasant? A certain driven, obsessive quality develops in our lives that is generated from constant seeking and avoiding. This becomes a purpose of our lives. Where are the happiness, joy and freedom in that?

When we meditate, however, we gain a new perspective on those people, places and situations we subjectively consider good, wanted or pleasant, bad, unwanted or unpleasant, or neutral. We gain some objectivity, so what we consider good, wanted or pleasant or bad, unwanted or unpleasant, no longer totally drives us. This allows us to be led by our Higher Power. We can begin to see the person, place or situation more *as it is* without imposing on it the distortion of our opinion. Meditation can be

> a level of functioning where we do not grasp onto our experience as it flows by, where we do not try to block things out and ignore them. It is a level of experience beyond good and bad, beyond pleasure and pain. It is a lovely way to perceive the world, and it is a learnable skill. It is not easy, but it can be learned.[61]

Here is a story about how our opinions and concepts can affect our teachability.

After the meeting, the Newcomer approached the Oldtimer who was standing by the coffee pot to discuss his personal theories about recovery. The Oldtimer poured the Newcomer a cup of coffee until the cup was full and then he kept on pouring and pouring.

The Newcomer watched the coffee overflow until he no longer could restrain himself. "The cup is full! It won't hold any more!"

The Oldtimer said, "You remind me of this coffee cup. You are full of your own opinions, theories, and speculations. How can you learn anything about recovery unless you first empty your mind?"[62]

CHAPTER 14

Difficulties with Meditation

The experienced and committed aspirant will sooner or later come to realize that the ego is fighting for its existence. It will go to any extreme to survive.

—David A. Cooper

We face difficulties with meditation as with any other endeavor. The difficulties of meditation are unique because the act of meditating creates "difficulties" something like the body creates antibodies to fight off medicine. Our self-perpetuating identity (ego) will go to any length to maintain itself, not to be penetrated, not to have its constructed nature exposed. Meditation can be difficult, not because we are inept at this spiritual technology but because it threatens our sense of who we are.

A skillful meditator knows and recognizes factors that are hindrances to his meditation practice. These hindrances are mental obstacles that arise and pass away during meditation that interfere with the primary goal of 11th Step meditation — improving conscious contact with our Higher Power. Since these same difficulties or hindrances arise off the cushion, the skills we learn by dealing with them during meditation are easily transferable to our daily life.

Our lives don't work because we aren't working at it and working at it means we have to work with our difficulties.

Five Hindrances.

Traditionally there are five mind states that are hindrances to meditation:

- **desire** (seeking, wanting, greed, grasping or lust)

- **aversion** (ill-will, hate, fear, resentment, rejection, or judgment)

- **sleepiness** (sloth, lethargy, laziness, torpor or dullness)

- **restlessness** (anxiety, agitation, impatience, worry and excitement)

- **doubt** (uncertainty, loss of direction, lack of confidence, hesitancy and questioning)

The manner in which these mind states or mental factors hinder our meditation is that their presence distracts awareness from the primary focus of meditation, which is normally the breath and breathing. The extent to which one of these mind states operates to hinder our meditation is directly proportional to how attached we are to the hindering mind state itself — great attachment creates great hindrance; moderate attachment creates moderate hindrance; slight attachment creates slight hindrance; and no attachment creates no hindrance. The arising of hindrances is as inevitable as breath or thoughts; their passing away is inevitable, too. As long as they are present, they can dominate our entire field of awareness.

Using Hindrances.

A fascinating paradox of meditation is that these hindrances themselves can actually help us in our meditation, just as weeds can nourish plants when they are plowed back into the soil.

The technique to deal skillfully with intrusive hindrances during meditation is to *transform* them into the object of meditation until they no longer dominate the field of awareness. We can do this by recognizing the hindering mind state when it arises, using the labeling technique (such as "wanting, wanting," "doubting, doubting," or "thinking, thinking"), and then by not clinging, not rejecting, not identifying with that mind state. The key point is to lightly notice the hindrance, but not to control it, grasp it or push it away.

Let me give an example how this might work. Suppose it is 7:00 on a lovely, quiet summer Sunday morning. Let's say I am meditating, following my breathing as the focus of awareness. Suddenly right outside my Meditorium window, my neighbor cranks up his lawnmower. Baarrrrrruumbadaaa! Baarrrrrruumbadaaa! I assure you this has happened often. Before recovery and a regular meditation practice, I might have had something like the following internal monologue or story line:

> The lawnmower! Oh, no. He's gonna mow his yard! Now? Damn it! I'm trying to meditate. And it's 7:00 on Sunday morning. Doesn't he have any consideration for his neighbors? Now I can't meditate. It's too noisy. I can't concentrate. How can I meditate? I should meditate, but I can't. Oh, hell, I'll just meditate later, when it's quiet, when the conditions are better. Yeah, later.

I then would have stopped my daily meditation, up, telling myself "I'll do it later when conditions are better." I would probably keep putting meditation off for "later" until it was too late that day and I would just blow it off for the day, maybe for a few days, maybe even forever.

That was then and this is now. This is much more like the internal process I would commonly have now:

> The lawnmower. *Oh, well. Hearing, hearing.*

And I would return to the focus of awareness to my breath and breathing. Notice a recognition of the hindrance, followed by a labeling of the nature (but not the content) of the hindrance, and then a return of awareness to the breath.

Sometimes it's not quite so easy, but it is still simple. A telescoped summary how my internal story line might play out if I am having trouble letting go of the hindering lawnmower is:

> The lawnmower. *Oh, well. Hearing, hearing.* He's gonna mow his yard! *Anger, anger.* It's 7:00 on Sunday morning. *Thinking, thinking.* Doesn't he have any consideration for his neighbors? *Wait, it's anger.* Why did he buy such a loud lawnmower anyway? *It's just a noise. I'll shift the focus of awareness from breathing to anger. What does the anger feel like in my body? Noticing, noticing. The front of my chest and my throat are tightening, right there, and I feel a spurt of adrenaline here. Feeling, feeling.*

Now I can probably return my focus to breathing. If not, if I am really getting wrapped around the axle, then I continue to observe and experience the physical sensations associated with the feelings, using the labeling technique occasionally. I might gently and silently remind myself that the feelings which, like clouds drifting past a mountain, will arise and pass away.

Instead of condemning our hindrances, learning to use them as nourishing "mind weeds" improves our capacity to accept and love.

> A man who took great pride in his lawn found himself with large and recurring crops of dandelions. Although he tried every method he knew to get rid of them, they continued to plague him. Finally, in desperation, he wrote the Extension Service of the Agriculture Department of the State University, enumerating all the things he had tried and concluding with the questions: "What shall I do now?"
>
> After a somewhat prolonged time even for such correspondence, the reply finally came: "We suggest you learn to love them."[63]

Part Three
Meditation and the Program

CHAPTER 15

Change

If you try to base your happiness on things that change — sights, sounds, sensations in general, people and things outside — you're setting yourself up for disappointment, like building your house on a cliff where there have been repeated landslides in the past. So true happiness has to be sought within. Meditation is thus like a treasure hunt: to find what has solid and unchanging worth in the mind, something even death cannot touch.

—Ajhan Thanissaro

Change is what happens with everything at all times. People in recovery often say they have difficulty with change. To the extent this is accurate, this means we have difficulty accepting life's most fundamental characteristic. How can we be happy and sane if we are at odds with the way things really are? Meditation can be conceived as a technique to investigate, experience and accept change.

Change and Impermanence.

Heraclitus, the Greek philosopher who lived around 500 B.C., recognized the pervasiveness of change and impermanence of the world. He is famous for such sayings as:

- all is flux, nothing stays still
- nothing endures but change
- you cannot step twice into the same river

If we observe objects, both natural ones (like people, plants, mountains, clouds and stars) and man-made ones (like tools, cars, buildings, airplanes and cities), we realize they all constantly change and are impermanent. These changing objects are *verbs* as much as they are *nouns*. Change happens faster (fruit flies) or slower (mountains) depending on the nature of the object, but change is nevertheless continual and inevitable. Subatomic particles and processes that comprise objects are themselves constantly transforming and changing at unimaginable speeds and in unimaginable ways. Modern physics teaches that matter and energy are equivalent, merely different forms of each other. Matter continually transforms into energy, and energy endlessly transforms into matter. This change is the universal dance of arising and passing away, illustrating the fundamental fact of change and transience.

Some people perceive, to a greater or lesser extent, their Higher Power as change, flow, process and transience, seeing all change manifest in the world as beginning, middle and end; as creation, enduring and dissolution; as arising, existing, and passing away. This underscores the Program saying that "God is a verb."

The changing and transient nature of reality become clear, perhaps startlingly so for some, when we meditate. Two insights quickly come to new meditators. First, we become aware through meditative observation that a waterfall of sensations, feelings, thoughts and mind states constantly occurs — much of it previously unconscious to us. Second, we become aware that these myriad mind/body processes are transient — they continually arise and pass away, one after the other, in ever-changing succession. Meditation demonstrates unequivocally on a visceral, experiential level that we are not fixed spiritual, mental or physical *beings*; rather, we are spiritual, mental and physical *processes*, where each element constantly arises and passes away.

Before we began to meditate, we knew *intellectually* that everything changes and is impermanent. Meditation transforms that knowledge into *insight* or *wisdom* through our experience of becoming intimate with the change at a depth at which before meditation we had no access. Change and impermanence are no longer concepts known only intellectually; they are processes that we have experienced.

Denying Change.

The very notion of "denying change" is absurd, but that is what many of us try to do. We do not like change or perhaps what comes along with change. Sometimes this is true even if the way things are is subjectively "bad," "unwanted," or "unpleasant." We just want things to stay the same. "Better the devil we know that the one we don't." It has been my experience that a primary cause of unhappiness and suffering is our attachment to that which changes. Very often this excessive attachment happens through self-deception by reification and deification.

When we *reify* something, we regard an abstraction (such as an opinion, belief, relationship or symbol) as a material, solid or concrete thing. The most common example is mistaking a *name* for something as the thing itself, such as confusing the word "God" for the living reality intended by the word. Another example is that if, say, I oppose flag burning, it means I have somehow come to regard an object (the U.S. flag, a symbol) for the underlying reality (the United States or its principles).

> You may think about things so much that you get into the state where you are eating the menu instead of the dinner, you are valuing the money more than the wealth, and you are confusing the map with the territory.[64]

When we reify a situation, we act as if the situation were solid and changeless, when of course it is not. When we do this, we are not living in reality. I reified my first marriage by mentally turning it from a living, dynamic relationship in process into a thing, a noun that I tried to manipulate and control. In doing this, it could not survive. So reification is forgetting that there is a difference between things themselves and our concepts of them — things are alive, while our concepts are static.

When we *deify* something, we make it our Higher Power, or at least one of them. Haven't all of us made Higher Powers out of alcohol, drugs, other people, gambling, sex, money, food, power, fame, whatever? We have made idols of them. We can all see the folly of this, sometimes even when we are in the middle of doing it, but even then we sometimes can't manage to figure a way out. Unhappiness and suffering comes from deifying something other than our Higher Power.

Reification and deification both illustrate our tendency to deny change, to mentally congeal living processes, to convert living, pulsating verbs into solid and dead nouns. When reality is recognized as a verb, as a process, we see how limited or absent our control over it is. When reality is seen as a noun, we imagine it is like a chess piece we can move around the board at our will for our advantage. Trying to hold on to things in this manner

> is like falling in love with a beautiful river and trying
> to take it home in a bucket.[65]

Much unhappiness derives from futilely attempting to freeze or hold on to a person, place or situation, acting as though, despite all evidence to the contrary, it will not change. Our vain attempt to keep things from changing is the greatest source of pain and suffering in our lives.

I become unhappy and suffer when I reify and deify a person, place or situation. For instance, at first I am happy having a new relationship with a woman and letting it just happen. At first. Before long, however, I begin to reify the relationship into a noun; and I often deify the woman into a Higher Power. In doing this, I plant seeds of destruction, because it is inevitable that the relationship will change. I treat the changeable as unchanging and so I become unhappy and suffer when it changes.

Meditation erodes our inclination to reify and deify by proving in our very mind's eye that what we otherwise might have tried to reify or deify is changing, transient and essentially insubstantial. "Life is but a dream" means we are only dreaming if we think of reality as a still life. When we realize this on a gut level, we can let go of so much of it because we see there is no other rational choice. I can serenely let go; the only question is whether or not there will be claw marks.

We spend so much psychic energy trying to put everything in its proper place, to make everything solid and secure. When we finally become willing to step out into the unknown, uncharted, and shaky, then we are truly in recovery.

If we only realized that our objects of concern are transient and subject to change, we might live in closer contact with our Higher Power.

Several children were playing at the beach one afternoon. They each made sand castles. There were arguments over whose castle was the strongest, biggest and best, with stern warnings to stay away from each other's castles. Late in the afternoon, one of the children kicked over another child's sand castle, fists flew, and a melee erupted.

When evening came and it grew dark, it was time for the children to return home. No one now cared what became of his castle. One child stamped on his, another pushed his over with both hands. Then they turned away, each to his home."[66]

CHAPTER 16

Detachment and Letting Go

Letting go is a central theme of spiritual practice.

—Jack Kornfield

We talk a lot in the Program about detachment and letting go. Sooner or later we come around to understanding that detachment and letting go are great solutions. But there is this one small problem — how do you actually *do* it? How do you learn to detach? How do you learn to let go? Meditation specifically trains us in detaching and letting go. And when we can't let go, we simply observe how we hold on.

Detachment and Letting Go.

A basic feature of insight meditation is watching the experience of the breath and, when sensations, feelings, thoughts or mind states intrude into the field of awareness, noting that and then detaching from them and letting them go. By doing this with each sensation, feeling, thought and mind state, we become better able to detach and let go of people, places and situations (actually the sensations, feelings, thoughts and mind states associated with them) in our daily lives because we have trained ourselves in doing so. During a typical 15-, 30- or 45-minute meditation period, we practice detachment and letting go *dozens* of times, on a sensation-by-sensation, feeling-by-feeling, thought-by-thought, and mind state-by-mind state basis. This highly concentrated training in detachment and letting go can be contrasted with a normal day without meditative awareness, when we might consciously practice detaching and letting go just a few times, if at all. Imagine the cumulative effect of concentrated training in detachment and letting go over several days, weeks, months and years. In this way lies liberation from enslavement to our own desires and aversions.

Letting go really means choosing to become transparent to the strong pull of our own likes and dislikes, and of the unawareness that draws us to cling to them.

In addition to the practice in letting go of sensations, feelings, thoughts and mind states, meditation teaches us on an experiential level that all these mind/body experiences arise and pass away. They are impermanent. This experiential wisdom lessens our tendency to hold on to them in the first place, understanding the futility of attachment to that which is transient. Letting go is not so much an act of will as it is recognition of the inherent transience of all things. And when we can detach and let go of what changes, we recover and liberate our true nature.

It is not "wrong" to have attachments; that kind of thinking only leads to more suffering. Rather insight meditation teaches us to look deeply at our attachments. We ask ourselves not only what do I attach to, but how does attachment actually work and does it bring me what I deeply want? Asking these deeper questions gives us the insight that allows us to let go.

Letting Go of the Good Stuff.

Usually we think of detachment and letting go as pertaining to difficult or unpleasant things, such as the letting go of the addictive behavior of others or distressing situations over which we are powerless. This makes sense because we don't want them anyway! But we must also keep in mind recovery also derives from detaching and letting go of that which is pleasant and enjoyable. This may sound a little counterintuitive and even radical, but let me explain. Just as newborn puppies must not be over-handled, consider this illustrative quote from William Blake's *Eternity*:

> He who binds to himself a joy
> Does the winged life destroy
> But he who kisses the joy as it flies
> Lives in eternity's sun rise

If we attach to or hold on to that which is pleasant or enjoyable, we may damage or destroy it and possibly even convert it into a Higher Power. Doesn't the alcoholic attach to her alcohol? Doesn't the addict cling to his dope?

Shinzen Young once reduced this principle to a formula:

$$satisfaction = pleasure \times equanimity$$

Pleasure treated with equanimity will generate more satisfaction than pleasure which is grasped and held. Remaining emotionally sober over what is pleasurable rather than going off the deep end in a mad scramble to maintain the pleasure or infinitely repeat it serves to enhance the pleasure. Losing our composure over what we find pleasurable ultimately leads to diminished satisfaction.

Letting go of everything — that which is painful and that which is pleasurable — just letting things be what they are, is not what we are taught in our culture. But has the norm worked well for us so far? The more we can let go, the more peace and freedom we will attain.

This story about two celibate monks illustrates an instance of detachment and letting go.

Tanzan and Ekido were once traveling together down a muddy road. A heavy rain was still falling.

Coming around a bend to the crossroads, they met a lovely girl in a silk kimono and sash, unable to cross because of the deep mud.

"Come on, girl," said Tanzan at once. Lifting her in his arms, he carried her over the mud.

Ekido did not speak again until that night when they reached a lodging temple. Then he could no longer restrain himself. "We monks don't go near females," he told Tanzan, "especially not young and lovely ones. It is dangerous. Why did you pick up that girl and carry her?"

"I left the girl back there at the crossroads this morning," said Tanzan. "Are you still carrying her?"[67]

CHAPTER 17

Pain and Suffering

[S]uffering is what happens to us when we want something other than what is.

—Cheri Huber

Why discuss pain and suffering? Isn't that a bit unpleasant? The fact is we all come to 12-Step recovery because we want relief from our pain and suffering; pleasure, delight and joy aren't what got us in the door.

Pain is Inevitable; Suffering is Optional.

A Program adage is "pain is inevitable, but suffering is optional." What does this mean? To me it means pain is inherent in our human existence, an inevitable part of life's terms, but suffering is optional because it arises from resistance to pain.

There are all kinds of pain. The basics ones are: birth, disease, old age, death, not getting what you want, losing what you have, and getting what you don't want. Pain has many faces ranging all the way from a stubbed toe to deep existential anguish — from a lost toy to a discovered affair, from fear of intimacy to boredom with a marriage, from disappointed career expectations to grief over a parent's death, from uncertainty about a business deal to a nagging sense of dissatisfaction with our lives. Pain is inevitable because it is part of life.

As long as we deny that pain is inevitable in our lives ("But wait! That's not fair! I shouldn't be experiencing this pain. This is not my correct life experience."), we will suffer. Suffering arises, in other words, when we fight against pain, when we resist it, when we try to interfere with it. Suffering arises out of the crazy notion that we want to try to make life to be other than it is. We seek solidity and control, but what really happens is that solidity and control turn out to be the cause of what we seek to dispel. In yearning for pain to be assuaged in such ways, we reinforce what creates suffering in the first place – the craving for life to be other than it is.

We will always have pain in our lives, but *we will not suffer if we do not resist pain*. We mistakenly believe that by resisting pain we can protect ourselves from it, when in fact resistance is the source of our suffering. If you look closely, you will see that we increase our suffering when we tighten around it.

Shinzen Young once reduced this principle to a formula:

$$suffering = pain \times resistance$$

Meditation provides a way to sit and face our pain, however it presents itself and to practice not fighting it, not resisting it, not interfering with it. In this sense, meditation is counterintuitive. In meditation we observe and experience our pain and just allow it to arise and pass away. We don't avoid it. In this way we reduce or eliminate suffering by concentrating on the pain that is right there in front of us rather than creating suffering by thinking about how to avoid our pain.

> When we sit in meditation, our minds wander, and the way in which we return our attention to the present provides an instant display of how we deal with ourselves — and how we are with ourselves is how we are in the world. In observing with full acceptance whatever distracts us, and gently returning the attention to the present, we discover both what prevents us from enjoying the sufficiency of the moment and how to let go of that resistance to whatever is happening.[68]

If we are not willing to face our pain, we you will surely continue to experience suffering.

By diving into the pain in this very moment with this very breath, suffering does not arise and pain is processed. Meditation also prepares us not to resist pain and so not to suffer when we face painful life experiences in daily life.

> This practice involves finding a willingness to suffer
> in order to end our [pain]. Instead of spending our
> time trying to avoid [pain], we just find the willingness
> to go directly into it.[69]

One November I told my girlfriend I wanted to end our relationship. She asked me to delay the breakup until after the Christmas holidays. More than two years later our relationship ended. I avoided the brief period of the pain of an immediate breakup in return for two years of suffering (not that it was all suffering). We talk in the Program a lot about willingness, and part of that willingness is to face our pain rather than avoid it. This technique has general application to our lives. The way in which we learn to sit with our pain and observe precisely how we deal with it can apply to our entire daily lives.

> Spiritual practice will not save us from suffering and
> confusion, it only allows us to understand that
> avoidance of pain does not help.[70]

Each time our mind wanders in meditation, the way we deal with it is our own personal demonstration of how we deal with similar situations off the cushion. If we can simply accept our distraction and return our awareness to the breath and breathing, we can learn what prevents us from enjoying the sufficiency of the moment and how to let go of that resistance to whatever is happening.

Going Farther, Faring Worse.

People in recovery often lament that they have been working hard at the Program but, damn it, things are getting worse, not better. What is happening here? What have we gotten ourselves into? One Asian spiritual tradition calls this "going farther and faring worse." It is not that we are getting worse at all. It is only that we are beginning to see and feel what actually is there, what we have so long denied. Now what? The answer is the Program saying that, "The only way out is through." So often we must face the onion in tears even as we peel away its layers.

The reason is that we are undertaking the heroic journey of experiencing pain we used to avoid. But the only way out is through.

Pleasure and Suffering.

Our 12-Step rooms are filled with people who suffer over their pleasures. As with detachment and letting go, a corollary to the principle that resisted pain leads to suffering is that grasped pleasure is ultimately unsatisfying and often leads to addiction, obsession, compulsion, and drivenness. The only pleasure that is satisfying is pleasure which is not grasped but is completely experienced and then released. Hence meditation teaches us on a sensation-by-sensation, feeling-by-feeling, thought-by-thought, and mind state-by-mind state basis not to grasp pleasure.

This woman is so unwilling to face the inevitability of pain that in seeking to avoid it she suffering greatly.

> Once in a village, a woman's small child suddenly died from illness. Distraught, the woman ran to the Buddha and asked for his help.
>
> "Give me medicine to bring my son back to life," she begged.
>
> The Buddha, seeing the woman was ripe for understanding, said, "Go back to the village. In whatever house where no one has ever died, bring me a few grains of mustard seed from that house."
>
> The woman rushed back to the village. For hours she went frantically from house to house asking if anyone who had lived in that house had ever died. In each house she heard a similar story. "My elderly father died last year." "We lost five here from the spring sickness." "The floods killed my husband." In each house, it was the same. "I am sorry, dear, but in this house someone has died."
>
> Finally the woman understood and she buried her son.[71]

CHAPTER 18

One Breath at a Time

Each moment is my best opportunity to see how I cause myself to suffer: what I'm believing, what I'm clinging to, what I'm pushing away that causes me to suffer.

—Cheri Huber

"Where have I been?" We have all had the experience while driving a car of suddenly realizing that we forgot the last few minutes of driving. We "awoke" from our driving amnesia and found ourselves in our car driving down the street with absolutely no memory of the last mile or so. Where was our mind during that time? Certainly not present where our bodies were. Lost in some memory, planning or fantasy. I believe this condition of being not-present or mindlessness permeates our lives much more often than we realize, certainly more than occasionally when we are driving.

In our normal state of awareness we cannot see the extent to which we are not-present, for the simple reason that being not-present is a state of unawareness.

Meditation teaches and trains how to wake up and realize the present moment, Here and Now. In a profound sense, what we are trying to recover *is* the Here and Now. But learning to be awake in the present moment is an elusive endeavor. One of the most difficult things to remember is to remember. Awareness begins with remembering what we tend to forget. And when we practice meditation long enough falling asleep begins to wake us up.

I once asked my friend Donna how she had enjoyed a pre-recovery European trip with her alcoholic/addict boyfriend. She didn't remember much about Europe, she said. During her European vacation Donna spent so much attention, mental energy and awareness concerned with what *he* was doing and what *he* was not doing that she was unable to be present enough to enjoy Europe. She barely remembers even being there. I am sure many of us can relate to this.

Much of my *life* before recovery was not-present, asleep. If we sleepwalk through life, we cannot expect to see very much. As Henry David Thoreau wrote, "Only that day dawns to which we are awake."

One Day at a Time.

I first used the Program principle "One Day at a Time" in 1987, before I came into recovery, when I started jogging. I knew the One Day at a Time principle from exposure to the Program through my ex-wife's AA involvement, but I had never used it.

It can be tough to stick to an exercise program, and I assumed running would be no exception. When I considered jogging "for the rest of my life," it was a daunting prospect. Like an alcoholic or addict facing the prospect of a lifetime of abstinence, narrowing my focus to jogging just for today eliminated resistance just enough to allow me to jog regularly. On the days that I did not want to jog, I reminded myself I could certainly run that day and not concern myself with the next day or any other day. The One Day at a Time principle worked for my jogging. Except very rainy days and illnesses, and until my heart attack, I did not skip more than thirty days of jogging over ten years. When I came into recovery in 1991, my successful experience with the One Day at a Time principle gave me confidence in it. From experience comes confident faith; from confident faith comes experience.

I use the One Day at a Time principle when it comes to daily meditation. A few times I have been reluctant to meditate. When this happened, I recalled I was working a Program of recovery that suggested meditation as one of its spiritual practices, that I was willing to go to any length to "get it," and that all I needed to do was meditate "just for today." It eliminated resistance. Since I started meditating in April 1992, I have not missed a single day, even the day I was hospitalized with a heart attack.

Many people say how difficult it is for them to stick with a meditation practice with any consistency. So I suggest that when you look at having a meditation practice you consider using the One Day at a Time principle. It makes perfectly good sense since, after all, we are trying to "practice these principles in all our affairs" (Step 12) on a daily basis.

The Present Moment.

Cutting our lives into one-day slices with the One Day at a Time principle makes facing our challenges more manageable. We can usually do for one day what might seem impossible to do for a lifetime.

A related 12-Step principle is living fully in the present moment, in the Here and Now. We are conditioned to avoid the Here and Now. Our minds wander to the past and its consequences, the future and its prospects or some fantasy — even if we are unaware we are doing so. Our monkey minds furiously swing back and forth among the branches of past, future and fantasy, grasping at the tempting fruit of desire. Another way we avoid the present by conceptualization. Rather than experience what is in front of us, we intellectualize it. We say, "That is a sunset" rather than saying "*Look at that sunset!*" To the extent we do this, we live in a dream world; we forget to be present. Meditation teacher Ayya Khema wrote, "If we live in forgetfulness, we die in a dream."

The Program encourages us to be in the present. My experience is that meditation is the sharpest tool for learning to live in the present since it involves *practicing* being in the present, in the Here and Now. In fact, there may be no better way to learn to live each moment than through meditation.

> The work of waking up from these dreams is the work of meditation, the systematic cultivation of wakefulness, of present-moment awareness.[72]

When we sit down to meditate, we are committing to the present moment. That is why the practice brings awareness to the breath and breathing — a process which occurs only in the present. When we realize our mind has wandered off from being in the present, we gently return awareness to the breath and this moment. We are training ourselves in present moment awareness. Where else can we live and change? Because like it or not, this moment is really all we have to work with.

This skill of being able to keep or return awareness to the present moment is applicable during daily life. For instance, when I jogged I wanted to appreciate (if not enjoy) the experience. To do this I had to "be present to win." I felt my feet landing on the pavement, my legs and arms pumping, my lungs working. I liked to take in my physical environment — the coolness of the air, the breeze, the smells and sounds along the route, the stars, sky, clouds, buildings and other people. I was in the present moment.

Often my attention wandered away from the Here and Now to the There and Then — "how much longer until I am finished," "look how *far* it is to the next intersection," rehashing events from the past, planning the future, engaging in imaginary conversations. When I used it, the skill of returning to the present I practiced in meditation transformed the There and Then into the Here and Now. When I became aware my mind was elsewhere and elsewhen, I gently and without judgment returned my awareness to the present moment, just as during meditation. Guess what? It worked. The technique of return applies to all aspects of our lives — relationships, career, talking, reading, working the Program, "in all our affairs."

Momentum develops after we have meditated a while so that with increasing frequency we abide in the present moment even when we are not doing formal meditation practice. One day while walking to lunch, for instance, I found myself standing in the shopping center near my office, just breathing in and out in the present moment, glorying in the beautiful day — clear blue sky, spring coolness, vivid flowers, lunch smells. I realized that one gift of the Program and meditation was that very beautiful day and my ability to present, open and available to it. Before recovery, I could not stand still and appreciate the world because I was already on my way from where I was physically to where I was headed. I mentally leaned forward into the future. No wonder I was off balance. So often we sacrifice the journey for the sake of the arrival.

"If only" thinking (that I will be okay or I will be happy *if only* this or that would or would not happen) limits my ability to appreciate my life as it is in the present moment. Pema Chödrön wrote that we deprive ourselves of the miracle of being in the present by always thinking that the payoff will happen when we get what we want. But the truth is that the only place we can experience a payoff is right now. We work with the present situation rather than a hypothetical possibility of what could be.

Beyond learning to enjoy and appreciate my life, there is a more important benefit to learning the skill of returning to the present moment — improvement of conscious contact with my Higher Power. Where else can I encounter my Higher Power except right Here and Now?

> . . . [w]e cannot be in the present and run our story lines at the same time![73]

Mindfulness.

Meditation cultivates mindfulness. What is mindfulness? When we are mindful, we intentionally pay close attention to what is in right front of us, becoming a mirror that simply reflects what's there. Mindfulness is awareness which notices without judgment, without decision and without commentary.

As with just about everything else in the Program, mindfulness is simple but it is not easy. It takes effort. I have spent a lot of time and effort trying to be mindful. When that doesn't work, I do the exact opposite, which is to see all the ways that I am *not* mindful.

Mindfulness strings together awakened moments of presence of mind, creating moment-to-moment awareness. Mindfulness is not thinking. Rather, it is precision and clarity of awareness, being extraordinarily attentive and conscious of what is happening right here, and letting go of results — even the most common of daily activities such as washing dishes.

> There are two ways to wash dishes. The first is to wash the dishes in order to have clean dishes and the second is to wash the dishes in order to wash the dishes.[74]

The difference between awareness and mindfulness can be stated this way. Awareness is like going out into the dark night with a flashlight. Mindfulness is when we turn our attention to where the light shines.

We do not listen to a symphony or read a book just to finish them. We want to experience the work in its fullness, its beginning, middle and end. We invest ourselves in each of the 12 Steps as we work them. A Step is not worked to complete it or to get to next Step, but to work that Step. Likewise, we do not meditate in order to count from one to ten or to follow the breath, but to train ourselves in being present in the Here and Now, in each moment as it arises and passes away. Meditation teaches us exactly how to do this.

Meditation narrows the focus of our awareness from its randomly dispersed (insane) state. First it establishes us in One Day at a Time. Then it moves us to the present moment. Mindfulness is a third level of refinement in which present moment awareness is expanded to continuing moment-to-moment participatory awareness of the ever-changing inner world and outer world. Mindfulness is being right there when the doorbell rings, when our children ask to play, when we are afraid.

Attaining mindfulness, even for short periods, creates a state of balance, harmony, equanimity, and serenity. Interestingly, a quality of acceptance and non-judgment simultaneously arises. Meditation is an act which teaches us to be in the present and that is where mindfulness occurs. That is why we use the breath. Mindfulness can only happen in the present moment; if you are thinking of the past, that is a memory. It is possible to be mindful of memory, of course, but such mindfulness can only happen in the present.

Mindfulness is critical to our recovery because it permits us to be conscious in our conduct, to break the dozens of unhealthy automatic conditioned responses, and to be open and available to improve our conscious contact with our Higher Power. But swimming against the stream of our conditioning can be difficult. Mindfulness requires effort and discipline for the simple reason that the forces that work against our being mindful, namely, our habitual unawareness and conditioning are well entrenched.

This story is told about the Trappist monk, Thomas Merton, who encountered a novice at a monastery.

> Once he met a Zen novice who had just finished his first year of living in a monastery. Merton asked the novice what he had learned during the course of his novitiate, half expecting to hear of encounters with enlightenment, discoveries of the spirit, perhaps even altered states of consciousness. But the novice replied that during his first year of contemplative life he has simply learned to open and close doors.
>
> "*Learned to open and close doors.*" The quiet discipline of not acting impetuously, of not running around slamming doors, of not hurrying from one place to another was where this novice had to begin (and perhaps end) in the process of spiritual growth. "*Learned to open and close doors.*" Merton loved the answer and often retold the story, for it exemplified for him "play" at its very best — doing the ordinary, while being absorbed in it intensely and utterly.[75]

CHAPTER 19

Awareness, Acceptance and Action

It can be a useful practice to just sit still and refrain
from reacting when things happen that we don't like.

—Kyogen Carlson

In recovery we speak of the Three A's — awareness, acceptance and
action — which are crucial to our ability to "change the things we can."
As we attend meetings, work the Steps, read our literature, and talk with
our sponsors and fellows in recovery, we gradually cultivate these Three
A's. As a dynamic part of the 12 Steps, meditation provides a unique
means to accelerate development of the Three A's through focusing with
laser-like precision on our sensations, feelings, thoughts, and mind states.

Awareness.

A recurrent recovery theme revolves around the two poles of denial
and awareness. Denial is a form of self-deception and self-delusion
— we do not admit or see what is there. Awareness is a form of self-
honesty and self-knowledge — we acknowledge and see the truth of
what is there. Sometimes that is much easier said than done.

Meditation is a powerful tool for the simultaneous erosion of
denial and the development of awareness. At its most basic level,
meditation is the intentional direct observation of our own sensations,
feelings, thoughts, and mind states, and the conscious cultivation of
awareness of them. The awareness is not ordinary understanding.

I am not a psychologist or a psychiatrist (although I visited
several through the years). I do understand, however, that one way to
conceive the mind is that it consists of two elements:

- *conscious mind* — that part of our mind of which we are normally aware, such as our thoughts, sensations, feelings and mind states

- *unconscious mind* — that part of our mind of which we are normally unaware, such as unremembered memories, instincts, motives, aspirations, conditioning, etc.

When we meditate, we become aware of our sensations, feelings, thoughts and mind states on a deeper and finer level, which eventually allows access to some of what was previously closed off in our minds, which was previously unconscious. Gaining access to our unconscious minds reveals unknown aspects of our personality, character and nature, so we can now have a deeper understanding of who we are.

Meditation also allows us to see some previously unconscious habitual patterns of thoughts and actions by causing, or allowing, them to become conscious. I think working the other Steps also accesses the unconscious, but generally a slower pace. The reason we want to know our unconscious mind is to improve our awareness of who we really are, so we can accept it and then take appropriate action to "change the things we can."

Acceptance.

Meditation cultivates acceptance. As we sit in meditation, we practice and train our minds to observe sensations, feelings, thoughts, and mind states as they arise and pass away, sensation-by-sensation, feeling-by-feeling thought-by-thought, and mind state-by-mind state. We do not judge, grasp or reject them. We simply acknowledge and accept them as they are, without praise or blame, letting them pass by like clouds drifting past a mountain. After a while our expectation that sensations, feelings, thoughts, and mind states will be something *new* and *different* begins to vanish and we learn to accept just what is. We simply erode expectations.

> The spiritual path works this way. It is a matter of wearing out all expectation.[76]

When we meditate and a sensation, feeling, thought or mind state arises that dominates the field of awareness (displacing the prominence of the breath and breathing), we become mindfully aware of it, label it and let it go. We are open and available to whatever arises, noticing how we relate to it. We start to develop a soft, spacious and accepting mind and heart. Judging, grasping or rejecting a sensation, feeling, thought and mind states is not acceptance. Meditation teaches us to accept whatever arises, without judgment, grasping or resistance. Otherwise, when we like what arises, we hold on to it; when we don't like it, we push it away. Neither holding nor pushing away is acceptance.

The awareness and acceptance developed in meditation are vital in our daily life off the cushion. Life is an unending series of wanted, unwanted and neutral experiences. Through meditation practice, we cultivate an ability to accept those experiences on life's terms. When we encounter unwanted experiences (such as pain, change, loss, disappointment, frustration, anxiety, fear, aging, sickness or death) in daily life, we know them intimately at a gut level and have the wisdom borne of experience to know how to deal with them. We have repeatedly practiced working with them and have trained our minds to handle them. We know they will pass away like drifting clouds. We know they are not solid and have no inherent power. We have practiced and learned to observe them and let them go. We more quickly recognize, "Oh, this is anger" or "This is disappointment." This is quite the opposite from avoiding the feelings.

Meditation allows us to begin to see deeply that so often we *chase* after what we want so we can feel good and we *flee* from what we don't want so we can avoid feeling bad. "The problem is we become slaves to this process."[77] Chasing and fleeing, chasing and fleeing — this is life on the run. Is this how we really want to live? How serene is life on the run?

Acceptance is standing our ground. It is not seeking to get what we want; acceptance is wanting what we get. We learn in recovery that it is not so much what happens to us (the content of experience), but how we relate to that what happens to us (the process of experience). The consequence of nonacceptance of life's terms is suffering. When we reject or grasp, we only waste mental energy fighting a hopeless battle against life's immutable terms. Most suffering comes from refusal to accept reality. If we can realize that wanted, unwanted and neutral experiences are all our teachers, then life becomes a continual adult education class in spiritual development, sensation-by-sensation, feeling-by-feeling, thought-by-thought, and mind state-by-mind state.

> Until we learn to accept
> we cling to things being
> the way they have been,
> or we wish they were,
> or want them to be,
> or hope they will be.
>
> We tense up all our muscles,
> dig in our heels
> and RESIST.
>
> Then we believe that the energy
> we have put into resisting change
> is actually maintaining the status quo.
>
> We actually begin to believe
> that we are holding things together.
>
> Then we draw the conclusion: I am in control.
> And that conclusion is an illusion.
>
> When we learn to accept everything
> that comes into our lives,
> we are free from
> the pain of resistance.[78]

Action.

With improved awareness and increased acceptance of whatever arises, we are less confused. Our true nature shows itself more deeply, more clearly, without the distortion of so much mind-chatter, desire and aversion. Precious mental energy is freed for more productive use, such as recovery. As valuable as this improved perspective is, its value is limited unless it manifests itself in the action we take. After all, our Program is not a philosophy or a theory; it is a spiritual program based on *action*. The Program is not something to believe; it is something to *do*.

Remarkably the Program is not especially concerned with traditional notions of "good" and "bad" or "right" and "wrong." It is concerned with morality and ethics primarily as they relate to the development of desired qualities such as serenity, courage, wisdom, generosity, discipline, patience, wise effort, acceptance, rigorous honesty, gratitude, kindness, detachment, compassion and love. If we truly seek these qualities, the basis of our ethics will be this: what thoughts, speech and conduct are most likely to produce these qualities for myself and others? For instance, which is more likely to produce serenity and a calm mind — lying or rigorous honesty? stealing or generosity? love or hate? harming or compassion? manipulation or speaking directly? We *experience* the truth in the axiom "virtue is its own reward" because we deeply realize practice of these traditional virtues promote serenity and a calm mind. We undertake virtuous action, not because some minister, guru, dogma or text tells us to do so, but because our own experience convinces us that it is in our best interest, and usually that of others, to do so.

We can call behavior that produces these desired qualities "wholesome" or "skillful"; we can call behavior that produces undesired qualities "unwholesome" or "unskillful." This is a simple, practical model of how to behave in the world.

Meditation cultivates conscious living and conscious conduct. It helps us live an increasingly awakened life by training to be awake in the present, in this very moment. Seeing others benefit from our skillful behavior confirms its virtue.

Skillful behavior is self-reinforcing. With greater serenity and a calmer mind cultivated by skillful behavior, our meditation will be more calm and focused. If our meditation is more calm and focused, our insights become deeper. As our insights become deeper, we are more likely to behave more skillfully, thus producing still greater serenity, a calmer mind. It is a virtuous cycle.

> Then our actions can come from a place of deeper wisdom, instead of from the superficial winds of emotion.[79]

When we are in the present, we have choices about how we will live our lives. Letting go is a choice. We learn to choose what is fundamentally appropriate, by not acting in ways that lead to unhappiness to ourselves and others, but rather in a way that will bring happiness and joy to ourselves and others.

> The choice is expressed when we practice letting go, abandoning, not acting on unskillful thoughts and feelings, knowing with wisdom that they will bring unhappiness to ourselves and others. In the same way we can choose to act on skillful thoughts and feelings, knowing with wisdom that it will bring happy results.[80]

Do you think this Oldtimer understood the Three A's? What other choice was there?

> The Oldtimer was traveling across a field while on vacation in Southeast Asia when he encountered a tiger. He fled, but the tiger chased after him. Coming to the edge of a cliff, he caught hold of the root of a wild vine and swung himself down over the edge. Trembling with fear, the Oldtimer looked down to where, far below, another tiger was waiting to eat him. He held on to the vine for dear life.

> Two mice, one white and one black, started gnawing away at the vine. The Oldtimer saw a luscious strawberry growing near him. Grasping the vine with one hand, he plucked the strawberry with the other. "How sweet it tastes!"[81]

CHAPTER 20

Willingness, Honesty and Openmindedness

We find that no one need have difficulty with the spirituality of the program. *Willingness, honesty and openmindedness are the essentials of recovery. But these are indispensable.*

—Alcoholics Anonymous

Working a good Program requires willingness, honesty and openmindedness. A fruit of working the Program is the cultivation of willingness, honesty and openmindedness when we realize that these qualities pays handsome dividends. This is another reinforcing virtuous cycle. Similarly, willingness, honesty and openmindedness are necessary to practice meditation while at the very same time the practice of meditation develops them. Another virtuous cycle.

Willingness.

Willingness means being inclined, favorably disposed in the mind or ready. If we are serious about our Program, we are willing to "go to any length" to do the work suggested by the Program. Meditation is as much a part of the Program as a 4th Step inventory, a 9th Step amends, or any other element. Are we willing to work the 11th Step? A major impetus in my willingness was the dissatisfaction, pain and suffering I felt when I came to the doors of recovery. Sitting down onto the meditation cushion expresses willingness and at the very same time creates it.

Just as we show willingness each time we go to a 12-Step meeting, make a Program phone call, clean up after a meeting, or read Program literature, we show willingness to work and grow in the Program every time we sit down to meditate. It is another way to "suit up and show up." The slogan says, "You must be present to win" and meditation teaches exactly that — to be present in the Here and Now is a win. Even if a regular meditation practice is difficult, we can be willing to use our very difficulties as part of our meditation. We can be "willing to be willing" to have a meditation practice, just for today. At the very least we can be willing enough to go to our meditation area and sit down and meditate for 10 or 30 seconds. Once we are there, we might find our resistance (a character defect) has evaporated or at least diminished to the point that we can do one of the spiritual practices that the 11ᵗʰ Step suggests if we want to recover. We must be willing to come back to this moment and to pay attention. We continue to be willing to be present to whatever happens.

> We continue to be willing to come back to this moment and to pay attention. We continue to be willing to be present to whatever happens."[82]

Honesty.

Ours is a Program of rigorous honesty, especially self-honesty. For many of us, our character defects and conditioning have limited our ability to be rigorously honest. This may be so for several reasons. Perhaps we've done something we don't care to admit or we're afraid to tell the truth for fear of the consequences. As we work the Program, our conditioned thinking and behavior changes; this is one thing our Higher Power does for us that we cannot do for ourselves. Then our ability to be honest improves as we learn to open up, we more clearly see our motives, and we see that honesty leads to the very spiritual healing we sought when we came to the doors of recovery. This process is experienced during and accelerated by meditation.

> Although it is embarrassing and painful, it is very healing to stop hiding from yourself. It is healing to know all the ways that you're sneaky, all the ways that

you hide out, all the ways that you shut down, deny, close off, criticize people, all your weird little ways.[83]

Meditation is an inherently honest act. If we sit down to meditate and do the practice, we must face ourselves honestly, exactly as we are — warts, beauty marks and all. We are honest when we meditate; if we are not, we are not meditating. We cannot "act as if"; we must be honest with what we find when we do the practice. Meditation is the practice of honesty and at the very same time we cultivate honesty when we face ourselves. The reason people don't want to meditate is that they are not willing to face what comes up.

Many people quit meditation practice for this very reason: it opens the door to everything we have tried not to face.[84]

Openmindedness.

Openmindedness is a good description for meditation. As we meditate, we openly face our feelings, thoughts, opinions, concepts and beliefs. We see them and we see through them to what they are — precious yet essentially insubstantial and transient. We just sit there — open to whatever sensations, feelings, thoughts or mind states arise. Our minds are like umbrellas; they work best when they are completely open.

Learning willingness, honesty and openmindedness requires practicing them, even if you are only "acting as if" at first. This story illustrates this principle about learning humility.

A man went to Wahab Imri and said:

"Teach me humility."

Wahab answered, "I cannot do that, because humility is a teacher of itself. It is learnt by means of its practice. If you cannot practice it, you cannot learn it."[85]

Chapter 21

Courage, Serenity and Wisdom

God grant me the serenity
to accept the things I cannot change,
Courage to change the things I can,
and wisdom to know the difference.

—Reinhold Neibur

The Serenity Prayer, which 12-Step Programs have adopted as their signature prayer, contains much of the Program's wisdom. We need courage, serenity and wisdom to work our Program of recovery; these very qualities are developed when we do. Likewise, it takes courage, serenity and wisdom to meditate regularly, and a regular meditation practice develops these qualities.

Courage.

I discussed in Chapter 1 (*My Story*) how my anxiety disorder brought me to recovery. When I came in the doors of the Program, I was regularly experiencing often debilitating anxiety and fear. At the time, I considered my fear to be cowardice. I was confused about what courage meant. I avoided situations that *might* precipitate a panic attack. Mild or intense periods of fear effectively paralyzed me. I thought courage would mean the absence of irrational fears. In recovery, I am learning that courage simply means *acting appropriately despite fear* — walking through the fear. This is still a great challenge for me, one that often I meet but sometimes I do not. I am grateful that today I usually accept my fear as an opportunity to grow, even when I find myself unable to walk through it.

As I worked the Program the first year or so, I saw with increasing clarity that my fear/avoidance cycle was a deeply conditioned response. By my own past behavior, I had conditioned myself to avoid or escape any situation in which I experienced, or *might* experience, fear. Recovery showed me that if I had become conditioned to act in an unhealthy way, then I could re-condition myself to act in a healthier, more skillful way. I could change! Many tools were available in the recovery tool chest, but for me meditation is the most effective tool for change.

Meditation is a safe, secure laboratory to re-condition myself by directly facing unpleasant feelings such as fear. When fear (or any other emotion) arises during meditation, the practice teaches me just to sit with it, to allow it to be there, to experience its nature, and watch it arise and pass away. There is no need to escape and no place to go. We do not distract ourselves from anything that arises when we meditate. We experience fear by sitting with it, allowing it to manifest and accept those feelings without running away. This process actually breaks down conditioning, which means cultivating courage by teaching us to face our fears in daily life off the cushion as well.

When we train our attention in meditation on fear (or any other emotion), especially the bodily experience and sensations of the emotion, its solid appearance is penetrated as we see it as a process that changes. Its grips is thereby loosened.

As with any strong feelings that arise during meditation, we note them and then focus awareness on the breath if we can, which causes the feelings to recede into the background of awareness. However, if the fear continues to intrude upon and dominate the field of awareness, then we simply observe and experience what the fear feels like in our body, closely watching those sensations arise and pass away. In this way, we learn courage through meditation.

Serenity.

I had a misconception about serenity when I came into recovery. I knew serenity meant a quality of dignified calm, peace of mind, and tranquility. I knew I wanted serenity. With my perfectionistic mind set, however, I mistakenly assumed that serenity meant being serene *all the time*. Since I was very far from serene all the time, this created a sense of failure, reinforcing my self-defeating belief loop that I had to be perfect to be lovable; I could not be perfect; therefore, I could never be lovable.

What I am learning in recovery is that human beings just do not have continual serenity. We all become upset and disturbed from time to time. However, what is possible and what I am learning one day at a time, moment by moment, helped by meditation, is the ability to *return* to serenity sooner after a disturbing event or circumstance. We all are bound to stumble at various places along the path, sometimes even falling, but regaining our balance as quickly as possible characterizes serenity. Meditation is a stabilizing gyroscope for the emotions.

Meditation directly influences serenity two ways. First, the regular practice of meditation is quite calming and settling in itself. This calmed, settled state of mind can persist throughout the day (especially if assisted by some off-the-cushion techniques described in Chapter 26: *In All Our Affairs — Life Off the Cushion*). Second, meditation generates insight to see deeply into the nature of our reality so that events or circumstances that used to be confusing or disturbing are either less so or no longer so.

Equanimity is an aspect of serenity. It is acceptance or noninterference with whatever arises from the five senses and in our minds, just allowing these sensations, feelings, thoughts and mind states to arise and pass away.

Wisdom.

Recovery teaches us the vital distinction between knowledge and wisdom. Knowledge is accumulated facts and information, which can be very useful in certain circumstances such as practicing law or building a bridge. Wisdom, on the other hand, is accumulated insight into the true nature of the way actually things are, undistorted by self-will.

All of us who have been in recovery for a while long ago lost count of the number of times we have heard someone say or read something during a meeting that is a Light Bulb Experience for us.

Sometimes it is a 100-watt "aha"; sometimes it is a 1-megawatt "AHA." Another term for each "aha" moment is "insight." Repeated insights leads to wisdom. The more insights we have, the more wisdom we develop. As insights accumulate, so does our wisdom until we "intuitively know how to handle situations which used to baffle us."[86]

What is curious is that so often these insights come from hearing something in a meeting we have already heard before, maybe dozens of times. I cannot explain why that is, but my intuition is that the time is right, we are just ready and we have accumulated enough wisdom that at least we are wise enough to listen and hear. The *knowledge* we have heard before suddenly ripens into *wisdom*.

Meditation leads to wisdom because meditation is an experience of *insight*. Meditation temporarily disengages normal cognitive thinking. Insight is intuitive, not conceptual. Somehow meditation creates readiness. Just as each scientific breakthrough has dozens, hundreds or thousands of applications, each insight generates dozens, hundreds or thousands of "applications" in our lives which lead to wisdom.

If a Program member or my sponsor has a certain gem of "wisdom" and he tells me about it, for me it is his "belief" but not my "wisdom," *unless and until* it becomes part of my own experience, strength and hope. If it were otherwise, we would not have to go to meetings and work the Steps; we could just read about recovery in a book. We have to live recovery and to make it part of our own experience for it to become vital and to usher in the recovery we all seek.

No one can *give* wisdom to us, we have to discover it for ourselves after a journey through the wilderness which no one else can make for us, which no one can spare us.

A meditation teacher said that, "wisdom is the gradual dismantling of that which does not work." What *doesn't* work for us are our character defects, because they block us from being happy, joyous and free. Meditation is a process of erosion of character defects, purification by seeing them for what they are. Meditation is uncovering our true nature by peeling off the onion layers of character defects, shortcomings, mind chatter and self-will. But we must act if we want the results.

> We don't get wise by staying in a room with all the doors and windows closed.[87]

Whatever the source of our insights, their value is determined by whether they are useful.

> Once a monk was digging in the garden at the monastery and came upon a very ancient piece of pottery inscribed in a language unknown to him. He took the pottery shard to the old Master and asked, "Can you translate this?"
>
> "Yes, I can," replied the Master.
>
> The monk asked, "What does it say?"
>
> The Master said, "Why are you looking for more knowledge when you do not pay attention to what you already know?"

CHAPTER 22

Actions and Consequences

A wise person is concerned about what he causes, but
not about what he receives. A common person worries
about what he receives, not about what he causes.

—Avatamsaka Sutra

Recovery is about responsibility to ourselves and to others. Some of
the things we learn in recovery about responsibility are:

- that we are responsible *to* others, but (except our young
  children) we are not responsible *for* others

- that we are not responsible for the actions of others and
  their consequences — that their happiness depends on
  their own actions, not on what we may wish for them

- that we are responsible for our own actions and their
  consequences — that our happiness depends on our own
  actions, not on what others may wish for us.

We each are completely responsible for our own experience.

All our feelings, thoughts, mind states and actions — who we
are and what we do — have consequences. Recovery helps us learn
to change our attitudes and actions; as a result, our consequences
change. Meditation teaches us how to do this.

Instant Karma.

We hear in meetings that recovery is about giving up the hope of a
better past. This wonderful saying reminds us that we cannot change

our past, but it also implies we can change our future. *We can change our future.* What a life-altering concept! Each moment, literally each and every single moment, including this very moment, is a new beginning and a new chance.

> Everything that happens emerges out of the causes and conditions that preceded it. Everything we do now becomes a cause and condition for what later happens.

Are we awake and aware enough to drink from the holy grail of the present moment? Meditation slows us down, allowing us to deeply participate in each moment so we can take full advantage of each opportunity to change our consequences.

Primarily in the early years in recovery, we devote much of our process to "clearing up the wreckage of the past." Wreckage refers to the adverse consequences of our actions. We see this especially when we first make and share our inventory (Steps 4 and 5) and when we list and make amends (Steps 8 and 9). As we come to recognize the adverse consequences of our actions around whatever brought us to recovery in the first place, it dawns on us that by "practicing these principles in all our affairs" (Step 12) our consequences will change. And for the better!

I hear people in recovery say that in taking or not taking certain actions, they consider how that action would appear to their sponsor, on their next 4ᵗʰ Step or 10ᵗʰ Step inventory, or whether the action will require a 9ᵗʰ Step amends or a 10ᵗʰ Step admission. These skillful considerations are a way of "clearing up the wreckage of the future," which means that to the extent we follow the principles of the Program, the future will hold less wreckage with which we must contend. To me this is a lesson of actions and consequences, of instant karma. Karma "is nothing more than the momentum to continue our past patterns into the future."[88] And we can change it.

If insanity is "doing the same thing over and over again and expecting different results," then sanity is doing things differently so we will experience *different and healthier* results. Since it is true that "if nothing changes then nothing changes," then it is equally true that if something changes, things *will* change.

Meditation is direct, accelerated learning about actions and consequences on a sensation-by-sensation, feeling-by-feeling, thought-by-thought and mind state-by-mind state basis. With the increased awareness and acceptance generated by meditation, we live more consciously and intentionally. We are no longer conditioned robots, sleepwalking through life, reacting mindlessly to defective, outdated programming of 10, 20, 30, 40 or even 50 years ago. The improved conscious contact with our Higher Power we obtain through meditation leads to conscious conduct. Conscious contact leads to conscious conduct. Conscious conduct changes our consequences.

We acknowledge in recovery that we are powerless over our past, which we cannot change. By conscious living cultivated by meditation, however, we create a future over which, with the help of a Higher Power, we have considerable influence. To the extent we are awake and aware in each moment, we can act skillfully to create a future in which we will enjoy living. Meditation is a skillful way to develop conscious living.

> The development of awareness in meditation allows us to become mindful enough or conscious enough to recognize our heart and intentions as we go through the day.[89]

Whatever we think, say or do has consequences far beyond what we can imagine. That doesn't mean we shouldn't think, speak or act. What it means is that we should think, speak and act   carefully because everything, literally everything, matters.

When we meditate impulses and momentum from our past come to mind. We don't act on them, but we do shine the light of awareness on them. We simply allow "the surge of habitual impulses" to wash up onto the shore of awareness, where they just fade out instead of drowning us.

Nonfruitative Intention.

When we talk in the Program about "letting go of results," we are referring to nonfruitative intention — taking action because it is inherently wholesome or skillful in itself, not because of the fruits it may bear. We leave the results to our Higher Power. Meditation fosters nonfruitative intention, so that whatever action we take, the results can be a lesson for us because we are more inclined to be attentive and aware. In the Program, we sometimes say there are no bad decisions, there on only consequences. Meditation fosters nonfruitative intention, so that whatever action we take, the outcome will provide us with a lesson. If we are attentive and aware, we will learn what we need to do next. In this sense, there is no wrong decision. The minute we make a decision, we are confronted with our next teacher.[90]

That Moment.

Many of our actions are automatic, conditioned responses. Meditation has helped erode some of that conditioning so we have the opportunity to react appropriately and in real time. I am becoming more of an intentional actor in the present, not an automatic re-actor using an obsolete script from the long-gone past.

One way we can see this happen in our lives is in what I call "That Moment." That Moment is the brief instant between the occurrence of an event and my action in response to it. It is in That Moment that I have a choice whether or not, and how, to respond or react to the event. In That Moment I have the opportunity to respond mindfully, intentionally, and skillfully, instead of reacting mindlessly, thoughtlessly, and automatically. Recovery can be gauged by the duration of and refuge in That Moment. Before recovery, That Moment arose and passed away so quickly that I was unable to capitalize on it very often.

Meditation is a chance to practice allowing That Moment to arise and be recognized; and in recognizing it, to allow it to grow and thrive. By reducing or removing our self-will and our ego from a situation, we create an environment where our Higher Power's will can be present. We cannot force That Moment to come into being. Counterintuitive, letting go creates a vacuum into which our Higher Power pours. This is training ourselves not to force results. That Moment proliferates as meditation practice matures.

When we are aware of our motives and intentions, we then have the freedom to choose whether or not we want to act on them. By learning to become aware of our motives and intentions sooner, our freedom to act is enhanced. As That Moment becomes more frequent and longer, our freedom and our conscious contact with our Higher Power improve and becomes more frequent and longer.

Allowing Space.

Character defects limit us and close us off from living fully and presently in the world. They block us from conscious contact with our Higher Power. The 3rd Step prayer calls them the "bondage of self." Defects or shortcomings are the result of our habitual defensive walls becoming prison walls. In Japanese the word for "hell" is translated as "no space." When others in recovery share and demonstrate their recovery and freedom, I crave more spaciousness, to break out from behind the walls, and to find the recovery and freedom they have found.

I attended a 12-Step meeting in which a man was sharing about the recent death of his mother. At one point he became choked up, so he paused for about 30 seconds, which is a very long silence in a group setting. Then he resumed sharing. It was a beautiful group experience that would not have occurred many other places in our society. A group of about 60 adults sat together in accepting, loving silence for 30 seconds in what would normally be considered an emotionally awkward or uncomfortable situation. The group allowed this man to experience his feelings without anyone trying to help him, fix him or "make him feel better." And, equally importantly, by not helping him or fixing him, the group allowed each of us to experience our own feelings without doing anything to fix them or make them go away. This spaciousness is one blessing of the Program.

Very often we get so uncomfortable with our feelings that we are compelled to do something to fix them, to distract ourselves, to entertain ourselves, to numb ourselves, to do anything to make things in this very moment different. Meditation practice cultivates our capacity simply to sit quietly with feelings of all kinds and experience just what is in front of us, without judgment, expectations, reacting or running away.

> It is a transformative experience to simply pause instead of immediately filling up the space. By waiting, we begin to connect with fundamental restlessness as well as fundamental spaciousness.[91]

Our life is transformed when we just pause and wait, instead of rushing in to fill up the space. By patience, we begin to connect with our fundamental restlessness as well as fundamental spaciousness.

By sitting in meditation, we learn to refrain from rushing to fill every vacant or uncomfortable moment. Meditation develops a quality of not lurching for some diversion as soon as we feel bored or uncomfortable. It's the practice of not immediately filling up space just because there's a gap.

If we don't rush to fill these empty spaces in our lives, we find the emptiness fills with a vast divine potential, with openness, where nothing is lacking and nothing is in excess. We have the chance to experience what is normally hidden from us, which is our Higher Power, who abides in that gap.

Traditional wisdom tells us that we will reap what we sow. Watch what you plant!

> Once a farmer planted two seeds in the same soil: a seed of sugar cane and a seed of a neem tree, a tree which is very bitter. Two seeds in the same earth, receiving the same water, the same sunshine, the same air. Two tiny plants emerged and started growing. The neem tree developed with bitterness, while the sugar cane was sweet. Why? As the seed is, so the fruit will be.
>
> The farmer went to the neem tree, bowed down three times, walked around it 108 times, and then offered it flowers, incense, candles, fruit and sweets. Then he prayed, "Oh, neem god, please give me sweet mangoes. I want sweet mangoes!" Poor neem god, he couldn't give mangoes. If someone wants sweet mangoes, he ought to plant a seed of a mango tree. Then he need not cry and beg. The fruit he will get will be nothing but sweet mangoes. As the seed is, so the fruit will be.
>
> Our difficulty, our ignorance is that we remain unheedful while planting our seeds. We keep planting seeds of neem, but when the time comes for fruit we are suddenly alert, we want sweet mangoes. And we keep crying and praying and hoping for mangoes. This doesn't work.[92]

CHAPTER 23

Compassion

The path of compassion means to silence the roar of our own internal chatter so as to be attentive to the gestures, hints, declarations, and appeals of others.

—Stephen Batchelor

A gift of the Program is increased compassion. I lived so much in my head, intellectualizing life that my heart, and thus my compassion, were atrophied. Compassionate listening is an example. When before recovery someone told me his problem, I assumed it was my obligation to give advice and to try to fix his problem, whether or not he requested it or I even knew what to do. I did not realize that sometimes people just want to be heard. This is ironic considering that I have always felt that I was not heard or understood by those I loved the most.

Sometimes there's just nothing to be said and nothing to be done. At such a time, the deepest communication of all is just to be there.

Recovery teaches not to give advice unless someone specifically requests it, and then only reluctantly. (Encouragement, however, is always appropriate.) Sitting through thousands of 12-Step meetings where crosstalk of any kind is unacceptable has provided the opportunity to practice listening to others without giving advice or even commenting. One virtue of this is that the person sharing feels she is heard and she is in fact heard. Another virtue is that I must sit with and experience my own feelings, thoughts and mind states — no matter how uncomfortable — without talking to distract myself from them. This practice teaches acceptance and erodes conditioned, mindless reactive responses to feelings, thoughts and mind states.

> It is the unaware mind that breeds insensitivity to
> people and things, for it doesn't see and appreciate
> the value of things as they are, only seeing them as
> objects to be used in satiating one's own desires.[93]

Meditation practice has enhanced my ability to listen to others because it teaches me to listen to myself. To be a good listener, I must be present, open and available. Being present means my mind must not wander or drift off in some fantasy, story line or conceptualization while someone is talking to me. Being open and available is willingness to acknowledge and accept whatever feelings, thoughts and mind states arise from what is said by the person I'm listening to. This is exactly what happens during the practice of meditation. We cannot truly be present, open and available to hear others unless we are similarly there for ourselves. The more we can do this for ourselves, the more we can do it for others.

Real communication at the heart level is presence, just being there for someone else, nonjudgmentally, physically, emotionally and psychologically. When barriers arise, we only need to watch them arise and pass, so that we remain open and available, feeling our feelings but not being pushed or pulled around by them.

> Really communicating to the heart and being there for
> someone else . . . means not shutting down on that
> person, which means, first of all, not shutting down on
> ourselves. This means allowing ourselves to feel what
> we feel and not pushing it away. It means accepting
> every aspect of ourselves, even the parts we don't like.
> To do this requires openness . . . not fixating or holding
> on to anything. Only in an open, nonjudgmental space
> can we acknowledge what we are feeling. Only in an
> open space where we're not all caught up in our own
> version of reality can we see and hear and feel who
> others really are, which allows us to be with them and
> communicate with them properly.[94]

Compassion vs. Pity.

We come to recovery in pain and suffering seeking relief. Not only can the Program provide relief if we just do the suggested work, but we receive the precious gift of compassion when we see that our own pain and suffering, as well as our joy and dreams, are essentially the same as those experienced by so many others.

The basis of real compassion is the insight that others are a kind of mirror image of ourselves.

Our sense of a connectedness with others creates compassion. As with the other qualities we have discussed, meditation creates and accelerates the development of compassion. Compassion has two elements: (1) sympathetic awareness of the pain and suffering of others; and (2) a desire to alleviate that pain and suffering. Pity only has one element: awareness of the pain and suffering of others. Pity differs from compassion in two respects: (1) pity lacks sympathetic identification with the sufferer, and (2) it lacks a genuine desire to alleviate the suffering.

Lowering the Shields.

I came into recovery highly defended and defensive, shielding my heart from what I considered untrustworthy people and dangerous situations in a threatening world. I liken myself to the Starship *Enterprise* when its crew incorrectly believed it was about to come under attack by an alien force which actually wasn't even in the same galaxy. I diverted most of my mental energy to maintaining my defensive shields at full strength, leaving little power left to run my engines to get where I wanted to go. I shielded and hardened my heart so I would be safe and would not be hurt. Or so I thought.

> We think that by protecting ourselves from suffering we are being kind to ourselves. The truth is, we only become more fearful, more hardened, and more alienated.[95]

By working a Program of recovery, including a daily meditation practice, I am gradually returning power from my shields to my engines as I come to see there is no real threat. I am not the target. My heart is flowering open, growing more soft and spacious. Acknowledging my own suffering and powerlessness, and being awakened to that of others, has been the gateway to compassion.

How does meditation develop compassion? In meditation we have a unique opportunity to see who we really are beneath our defense mechanisms and to experience those parts of ourselves we have long denied. We find that those hidden parts complete us, they don't destroy us. Because meditation creates an accepting awareness of sensations, feelings, thoughts, and mind states, we learn to be nonjudgmental of them, simply by allowing them to arise and pass away. Once we can do this with ourselves, we can be compassionate with others. From this compassionate core, we have a greater inclination to act — or choose not to act — in a compassionate manner that we deem skillful and wholesome under the circumstances. Skillful action is compassionate action.

> If we have the aspiration to stop resisting those parts of ourselves that we find unacceptable and instead begin to breathe them in, this gives us much more space.[96]

Compassion and interconnectedness with others erases self-centeredness.

> Time before time, when the world was young, two brothers shared a field and a mill. Each night they divided evenly the grain they had ground together during the day. Now as it happened, one of the brothers lived alone; the other had a wife and a large family. One day, the single brother thought to himself, "It isn't really fair that we divide the grain evenly. I have only myself to care for, but my brother has children to feed." So each night he secretly took some of his grain to his brother's granary to see that he was never without.
>
> But the married brother said to himself one day, "It isn't really fair that we divide the grain evenly, because I have children to provide for me in my old age, but

my brother has no one. What will he do when he is old?" So every night he secretly took home of *his* grain to his brother's granary. As a result, both of them always found their supply of grain mysteriously replenished each morning.

Then one night the brothers met each other halfway between their two houses, suddenly realized what had been happening, and embraced each other in love. The story is that God witnessed their meeting and proclaimed, "This is a hold place — a place of love — and here it is that my temple shall be built." And so it was. The holy place, where God is made known, is the place where human beings discover each other in love.[97]

CHAPTER 24

Discipline and Patience

Form a thought, create an impulse.
Form an impulse, create an action.
Form an action, create a habit.
Form a habit, create a destiny.

—Diamond Sutra

Spirituality requires nurturing. My spiritual experiences of the '60's eventually faded to pleasant memories precisely because I did not nurture them with regular spiritual practice, such as meditation. When I was in my twenties, I had no idea that, much like a garden, spirituality needs regular protection, nurturing and attention to live, let alone to grow and flourish.

A seed that sprouts can never be a seed again; it must have nourishment to grow or it will die.[98].

Sometimes maintaining consistency with a spiritual practice is difficult; perhaps at times it feels like a burden. But for those who are "willing to go to any length" to quench our suffering, finding the discipline and patience to maintain a spiritual practice such as meditation is crucial if we want what recovery offers.

Discipline.

Meditation is excellent discipline, like the discipline required for daily exercise or any other regular endeavor. Not only does meditation take discipline to practice daily, it cultivates and creates discipline by its very practice. Another virtuous cycle.

Some of us confuse discipline with strictness or severity. When we practice a discipline, whether it is meditation, getting regular exercise, or going to work, we can choose to see and appreciate it as a matter of our own choice and for what we perceive as our own good. Someone else does not impose it on us in response to his demands, needs or agendas.

The practice of meditation — a person sitting still with eyes lowered or closed — appears quite different from the outside than how the meditator experiences it. If someone were to see me meditating each morning, sitting with an erect spine, almost stock still for forty-five minutes, it might appear to be a difficult discipline. Yet on the inside, in the inner world of the meditator, what is happening is quite gentle and compassionate. It is practicing the skill of gentle, nonjudgmental return without expectation. Pema Chödrön writes:

> So on the inner level, the discipline is to return to gentleness, to honesty, to letting go. At the inner level, the discipline is to find the balance between not too tight and not too loose — between not too laid back and not too rigid.[99]

If we want to run a marathon, we have to train by running. If we want to paint portraits, we have to train by painting. It takes discipline to achieve our goal. Is the goal worth the effort to us? If we want to develop compassion and wisdom, to learn to let go, and to be fully present in this moment, to recover our true nature, we have to train by meditating and working the rest of the Steps. This, too, takes discipline. Is it worth it? Are we willing to go to "any length" to get what the Program offers?

Working our Program is a commitment to work a systematic spiritual practice within the framework of the Steps. A great deal of flexibility and diversity exists among various spiritual practices, but some skillful practice is necessary. How can we grow in the Program if we do not have the discipline to work the Steps? Unless and until we commit to the Program and meditation, how can we expect any results? The spiritual work of the Program requires sustained practice and a commitment to look very deeply into ourselves. If we do not stick with the Program, including meditation, in a disciplined way, we are never forced to face our own character defects. We are never brought face to face with ourselves.

> Until a person chooses one discipline and commits to it, how can a deep understanding of themselves and the world be revealed to them? Spiritual work requires sustained practice and a commitment to look very deeply into ourselves and the world around us. . .[100]

By learning to sit with whatever feelings, thoughts and mind states arise, to see them for what they really are, and to let them pass away, meditation creates the discipline not to distract ourselves when things get uncomfortable with alcohol, drugs, other people, food, gambling, sex or busy-ness. There is great wisdom in simply being with and accepting whatever thoughts or feelings would otherwise distract us, just resting in a place where there is nowhere we need to go and nothing we need to do beyond experiencing them. If we can exercise the discipline to remain

> right where we are, then our experience becomes very vivid. Things become very clear when there is nowhere to escape.[101]

When should we practice if not now? One of our most persistent illusions is that there is plenty of time to do what we need to do later, the kind of thinking that says this is just a dress rehearsal, that when things really count, *then* I'll do the right thing.

> . . . thinking that we have ample time to do things later is the greatest myth, the greatest hang-up, and the greatest poison. That, along with our continual, deep-seated tendency to try to get away from what we are doing, clouds our perceptions and our thinking.[102]

Patience.

Meditation takes patience, but it develops it as well. By sitting and watching our breath and breathing, letting feelings, thoughts and all mind/body processes arise and pass away, time after time, over and over, we become increasingly able simply to be with what is and not expect or need to change it. This is patience. Accepting what is exactly as it is. We disconnect our self-will or identity from the process of the arising and passing away of phenomena, a skill which comes in handy in daily life whether we are standing in a slow line at the grocery store or waiting for our summer vacation to begin.

> Do you have the patience to wait
> till your mud settles and the water is clear?
> Can you remain unmoving
> till the right action arises by itself?[103]

Like the Program generally, meditation is a process, not an event. A journey, not a destination. Be patient with your practice. There's just no hurry. Each and every moment is a fresh opportunity to begin to practice. During the seventh 45-minute sitting period on the third day of a four-day meditation retreat, the teacher said to us, "Forget everything that has happened in your meditation practice up until now. Start over right now." One beautiful aspect of the Program is that we have the opportunity to start all over every day of the week, every moment of the day, and with every breath we take. We discover and experience this constant beginning in meditation moment-by-moment, breath-by-breath. Knowing this, how can we be impatient when we practice meditation? Patience is not endurance; it is willing acceptance with each breath.

The Program generally, and meditation specifically, are like a curious spiritual treasure hunt. As long as we keep looking, we find what we seek; if we stop looking, it is lost. If we hang in there,

> . . . staying with it through [our] impatience and
> frustration and tiredness and disappointment when
> your expectations aren't met — sooner or later you
> will find what you are looking for.[104]

The patience we learn in meditation, which is not to expect or force anything, is helpful in all aspects of our lives off the cushion. If we meditate every day, we can become familiar and comfortable with our hidden qualities and our uncomfortable feelings. That's why we sit, so we can be more awake to who we are.

> That's why it's so good to meditate every single day
> and continue to make friends with our hopes and
> fears again and again. This sows the seeds that enable

us to be more awake in the midst of everyday chaos. It's a gradual awakening, and it's cumulative, but that's actually what happens. We don't sit in meditation to become good meditators. We sit in meditation so that we'll be more awake in our lives.[105]

If our spiritual practice is limited to meetings, the meditation cushion or church, we may not be prepared for life elsewhere. Patience is more difficult to practice around others than it is alone.

> Once there was a hermit who lived alone in a cave at the top of a mountain. He spent 20 years there developing patience, which he knew was vital to his spiritual path. His discipline was strong; he had practiced diligently. After 20 years the hermit decided he had perfected patience, so he left his cave and walked down the rocky mountain into the village below. He wandered through the village, fascinated by the familiar sights, sounds and smells of the busy marketplace. As he stood in line at a booth to purchase his first sweet in 20 years, a villager pushed into the line ahead of the hermit, stepping on his toes. The hermit became so angry that he hit the villager in the face with his fist.

CHAPTER 25

Problems and Solutions

When you are sitting in the middle of your own problem, which is more real to you: your problem or you yourself?

—Shunryu Suzuki

We all come to 12-Step recovery with some problem over which we are powerless and which has caused our lives to become unmanageable. That's why we show up at recovery's doors in the first place. Often a thunderstorm of disorientation or a fog of confusion engulfs us. The problem initially seems to be alcohol, drugs, another person or some other obsession or compulsion. We all want that problem to go away and, by God, we want that to happen now. Well, it just doesn't work that way. Although the Program is a time-honored solution, it takes time to counteract years of conditioned habitual unskillful thinking — stinking thinking — that caused and continued our involvement with the problem in the first place. Meditation gives us a new way of perceiving problems and solutions.

No Problem.

When we start attending meetings, we are amazed to hear people say they are grateful for the problem that brought them into the Program. Grateful for the problem? Alcoholism? Drug addiction? An eating disorder? This sounds insane to newcomers, who are usually firmly stuck in the middle of their problem and just want it to *go away*. Not only can't they see a solution, deep down inside they may fear there *is no solution* or certainly not one they can accept. When we were newcomers, sometimes we were so hopeless that it seemed we were totally alone with our problem in a frightening dark room without windows or doors.

What is it we learn in recovery that allows us to become grateful for the problem? We learn that it was our problem that led us to the Program and the Program not only gave us solutions to *that* problem, it also showed us a better way to live. One of the most common myths is that because we are alive we know how to live.

> The more we begin to understand that those sharp rocks on the road are in fact like precious jewels; they help us to prepare the proper condition for our lives.[106]

The problem became our teacher because we *learned to allow it.* Gratitude for the problem comes out of the willingness to open our eyes, our hearts, and our minds to it, to allow situations in our lives to become our teachers.[107]

Meditation is intensive practice in learning to allow feelings, thoughts and mind states to teach us and, by extension, to allow problems to be our teachers. What we think are stumbling blocks on the road of life are really precious jewels that help us see where we are stuck.

As the fog of confusion lifts, we learn with growing serenity that life is *always* going to have problems of one kind or another. "Getting it" in the Program includes realizing that recovery does not make problems disappear, but that we can transform them into opportunities to grow in a spiritually meaningful way. We learn that what we used to see as "problems" are not really our enemies, but our teachers. They show us where we are stuck. We learn that what we

> habitually regard as obstacles are not really our enemies, but rather our friends. What we   call obstacles are really the way the world and our entire experience teach us where we're stuck.[108]

If we do not avail ourselves of a particular opportunity to learn from a situation that we call a "problem", somehow that opportunity continues to present itself to us in one form or the other until we do. The longer we avoid facing the pain in the problem, the more we learn about suffering. Since meditation encourages and trains us in facing our problems directly, honestly and deeply, we suffer less.

Sometimes we find ourselves so completely caught up in a problem and its circumstances and its details that we feel lost and we do not know what to do. The Program provides many tools to become unstuck — attending meetings, talking with our sponsors or others in recovery, using the slogans like "Do the next right thing", reading the literature, doing service work, writing, praying, to name a few. Another way to become unstuck is meditation, which gives us distance, objectivity, perspective and clarity.

We can use difficult situations and unfavorable circumstances as opportunities to wake up and improve our conscious contact with our Higher Power. Just because we are in a situation we do not like does not mean we have to be upset about it. We can liberate ourselves from enslavement to our feelings, thoughts and mind states. In recovery we come to realize that everything that happens in our lives is not only "useable and workable but is actually part of the path."[109] This is clearly demonstrated and experienced during meditation as we sit with — not flee from — our problems or difficulties as they arise and pass away.

If we view a problem as an "enemy" which we either want to defeat or are unwilling to confront, we stay stuck there because we have defined and limited ourselves by the problem. Life is not so much a problem to solve as it is a mystery to behold. The Dalai Lama who, along with thousands of his fellow citizens, went into exile after the Chinese government overran Tibet and began a systematic destruction of its culture, called those same Chinese "my friends, the enemy." Surely there is a lesson for us there. When our thinking makes the profound shift from categorizing circumstances as good/bad or right/wrong into wanted/unwanted or skillful/unskillful, we are well on the way home. By changing our perception and attitude from one of judgment to one of acceptance (of the fact that the circumstance exists) through meditation and the other Program tools, we can begin to see a situation not as a problem, but as a *decision* in which we have the freedom of choice. We may not like our choices sometimes, but at least we have them. This makes problems easier to face and we then see that the best way to use unwanted circumstances on the path of enlightenment is not to resist but to lean into them. Befriending emotions or developing compassion for those embarrassing aspects of ourselves, the ones that we think of as sinful or bad, the raw material, the juicy stuff with which we can work to awaken ourselves.[110]

Success and Failure.

The Program teaches that when we do not succeed perfectly at a goal, even when we completely fail, we can learn from our experience and move on. We can "fail our way to success." We cannot do things perfectly and we don't have to. We come to realize that as humans we are imperfect, to accept that and be okay with it. That is why training our mind through meditation is so important. Each time our mind wanders during meditation (which we could consider a "failure"), we simply and without judgment return the focus of awareness to our breath and breathing (a "success"). Each breath is a new beginning, a new opportunity to face who we are, and return our focus to the Program and the practice.

In meditation, the concept of return is vital. When we have a slip in the Program, we do not quit. We begin again. After acknowledging what we have done (and taking appropriate action, such as making amends or doing an inventory, perhaps), we take the next right action. In meditation we do the same thing. Each time our mind wanders or drifts off, we acknowledge that and then return awareness to the breath. We do this thousands and thousands of times, one return at a time. In this way, we grant ourselves thousands and thousands of new beginnings, new chances. Repetition strengthens and confirms.

We all have problems in our lives. Despite this, somehow we have a sense that if we were only "doing things right," we wouldn't have any problems.

A man once came to the Buddha with his problems — his crops, the weather, his wife, his children and so forth.

"Oh, Awakened One, I beg you to put these problems aright."

The Buddha said, "I can't help you."

"But why not?" asked the astonished man.

The teacher explained, "Everybody has problems. In fact, we've all got 83 problems, each one of us. Eighty-three problems and there's nothing you or any of us can do about it. It's just the way life is. If you work really hard on one of them, maybe you can fix it — but if you do, another one will pop right back up in its place. If I *were* to remove one problem, another would just appear in its place."

"But then you can be of no help to me?" the man cried.

The Buddha smiled. "Perhaps I can help you with the 84th problem."

"The *84th* problem? What is the 84th problem?" the man asked.

The Buddha replied, "The 84th problem is that you don't want to have any problems."[111]

CHAPTER 26

In All Our Affairs — Life Off the Cushion

On the journey to happiness, you start anywhere.

—Sylvia Boorstein

By the time we have worked the 12 Steps the first time, most of us realize that these powerful Steps, the slogans and the principles of the Program apply to *all* our affairs — not just contending with alcohol, drugs, alcoholics and addicts, gambling, sex, food, keeping too busy or whatever substance or circumstance brought us into 12-Step recovery in the first place. The Program principles apply to our families, relationships, careers, education, recreation — in short, *all* our affairs. We come to realize that every aspect of our life is, or at least it can be, part of the recovery path. And it is not just that we *can* use the principles of the Program in all our affairs; it is that we *must* use them in all our affairs if we truly want to be happy, joyous and free. We can use the improved conscious contact with our Higher Power that we have generated during our daily formal meditation in all our affairs.

We spend most of our time outside meetings. It is in our daily lives that working the Program is the most difficult, challenging and useful. Being serene in 12-Step meetings is easy — it's a little different in 5 o'clock traffic, at cocktail hour with your alcoholic spouse, at Thanksgiving with a dozen of your closest relatives, or in the hospital emergency room. That is when we need the Program the most. In time we come to know beyond any shadow of a doubt that everything we do and everything we experience is part of our recovery practice.

The Program teaches that the details of each experience we encounter are not what is so important to our recovery; instead, it is how we relate to the experience and whether or not we can stay present, open and available to what is there. Meditation is actual "hands-off" training in staying present, open and available. We practice our Program when we meditate just as much as when we share in meetings, deal with an alcoholic or interact with our co-workers.

Off the Cushion Strategies.

Just as working the Program cannot be limited to being at 12-Step meetings if it is to be used to its full potential, meditation and a meditative attitude cannot be limited to the meditation cushion if we are to maximize its effectiveness. The compassion, wisdom and serenity we gain by daily meditation enrich our lives throughout the remainder of the day.

We can employ several strategies for daily periodic recharging our meditative batteries, whether or not formal sitting meditation is possible. Cultivation of mindfulness and serenity in all our affairs, in each moment, is at the heart of spiritual practice. When and where better to practice the Program than in daily life? Here are a few sample strategies for returning to the present:

1. Mini-Meditations. These are quick, thirty second or sixty second meditation periods we can do several times throughout the day when we have a spare moment, like waiting in line at the grocery store, on hold on the telephone, between tasks at work, at lunch, anywhere and anytime we have a moment to spare and to invest in our recovery.

2. Instant Labeling. We can use the labeling technique any time. Simply stop, look and listen for five seconds (or longer if you can). Ask yourself, "Where is my mind?" or perhaps "Where is my breath?" and then label your experience "thinking, thinking," "anger, anger," "wanting, wanting"? In this way, we develop and strengthen mindfulness. We can note where our mind is and simply let the feelings, thoughts or mind states arise and pass away, without grasping, rejecting or judging them.

3. Driving. A frequently overlooked opportunity for developing a mindful and serene attitude is when we are sitting, not on the meditation cushion, but behind the wheel of our automobile. Driving is a fantastic opportunity to practice staying present and aware, to observe what feelings, thoughts and mind states arise and pass away, without judgment or gaining idea. (Here I *strongly* recommend eyes-open meditation.)

4. Where am I? This technique is that every time we encounter a cue event of our choice (for instance a ringing phone, touching a doorknob, standing up, sitting down), we silently ask ourselves, "Where am I?", "Where are my hands?", "Am I inhaling or exhaling?" This brings us back to the present moment.

These simple strategies, and others you can develop on your own that work for you, are ways by which we can cultivate and strengthen mindfulness and serenity and at the same time recharge and improve conscious contact with our Higher Power on a daily basis. Meditation practice isn't just about sitting; every moment of our lives has opportunity to practice.

These techniques also increase appreciation of life by instantly transforming ourselves from a human doing into a human being, if only for a moment. I assure you that these moments will add up very, very quickly.

See For Yourself.

I love the fact that the Program does not require us to *believe* anything. Remember – the Program is not something to *believe*; it is something to *do*. The Program has certain principles, but the Traditions are clear that belief and dogma are not required for membership. 12-Step Programs are true spiritual democracies, open to all believers and nonbelievers alike. They encourage an attitude of "see for yourself." Experiment. See if this Program works for you. Do not take anybody else's word. We can learn from the experience, strength and hope of others, but we do not have to.

We can say the same for the benefits of meditation. In fact, a traditional admonition regarding the path of meditation makes this point clear:

> Believe nothing merely because you have been told it, or because it is traditional, or because you yourself imagined it. Do not believe what your teacher tells you merely out of respect for the teacher. But whatever way, by thorough examination, you find to be one leading to good and happiness for all creatures, that path follow like the moon the path of the stars.[112]

Like the Program itself, the path of meditation is not an ideology or dogma proclaiming the Truth, but a method of seeing who we are.

Although we in recovery have much in common with each other, we each have a unique personality and character. What works for one of us may not work for another; what works for us today may not work for us next week or next year. We have to approach our recovery life as an inquiring scientist or an intrepid explorer. The truth of the matter is that even though there are teachings and practice techniques, still we each have to find our own way.

We must remain present, open and available to adjust our Program to suit our changing needs. The Program generally and meditation specifically are flexible enough for that.

Easy Does It.

Like anything else, after you have practiced meditation for a while, it becomes more natural. All these meditation instructions are like a book on how to drive a car might seem to a twelve-year old. The instructions are confusing if you have never driven before. Once you have driven even a little, though, the instructions instantaneously become simpler and clearer. But remember no matter how many books you read, you cannot learn to drive a car unless you open the door, get in, turn the ignition on, place your hands on the steering wheel, put it in gear and press on the accelerator. Likewise, you cannot meditate unless you sit down and meditate. Just do it. The best teacher of meditation is meditation itself. And an interesting thing happens to your meditation practice as it matures. The more you practice, the less you need to do until finally you are just in acceptance. Because things are okay the way they are.

It must be clear from the fact that I have a daily meditation practice and that I have written a book about meditation and the Program that I value them and take them very seriously. Meditation means a great deal to me. I consider meditation *the* hidden jewel of our Program. Still, I believe it is essential to keep in mind that a sense of proportion, detachment, lightheartedness and humor is appropriate in working all aspects of our Program, including meditation. We mustn't take ourselves too seriously. And the fact is that if we treat the practice of meditation as a serious matter, a matter of consequence, then it will become embarrassing and heavy, overwhelming.

Meditation teaches us to live and appreciate life in each moment. Isn't it strange this is something most people are unwilling to do?

"How long is a lifetime?" asked the Master.

"Three score and ten," responded a student.

"Until you die," answered another.

"Both wrong," said the Master.

"How long is a lifetime, then?" asked the students.
"One breath," responded the Master.

"How can that be?"

"Because a person can only live one breath at a time. Yesterday's breaths are a memory. Tomorrow's are a speculation. The only lifetime a person can live happens within one breath."

"And what should we take from this?" asked the students.

"Respect the life you have when you have it. Live it. Be mindful of each moment during the moment. Instead of thinking about lunch, be present now. Feel the cushion under your bottom, smell the incense, see the vase holding the flowers."

"And what about unpleasant times?" asked a student.

"Then, too, be alive. Seek out the good moments among the less good. Even with pain, live with pain."

"This all sounds a bit odd," said one senior student.

"No, my friend," said the Master, taking a deep breath. "It is life."[113]

In Closing

May I respectfully remind you, life and death are of supreme importance. Time passes swiftly and opportunity is lost. We must strive to awake, awaken. Take heed not to squander your lives.

—The Buddha

I hope I have accomplished what I set out to do in this book — explain what meditation is, how to meditate, and how meditation relates to our 12-Step Program of recovery.

The incredible wonder of our 12-Step Program is that it teaches how to live — through the Steps, the slogans, sponsorship, literature, and the dozens of other tools we painfully and painstakingly learn to use. Meditation is an underused tool that could change the lives of everyone who practices it with modest diligence.

For me, the 12 Steps are a road map for the Road of Happy Destiny — a happy, joyous and free life. But to get where the map leads, we must work all the Steps, which includes meditation as suggested in the 11th Step. And when we are working all the Steps, we paradoxically find that each step along the path is our destination.

The Program, including meditation, worked well for me developing the beginnings of wisdom, compassion and serenity in times of joy as well as times of sorrow such as my Mother's illness and death and my Dad's cancer and death. But until 1997 there was always a nagging thought, "Yes, but will the Program and meditation work when *my* ass is really on the line?"

I am here to report the Program works when push comes to shove. I experienced a heart attack in July 1997. This was an opportunity to use the Program and meditation in quite serious and potentially fatal circumstances. For someone, a n y o n e, especially someone with an anxiety disorder, this heart attack could have been

Red Alert or Defcon One. It wasn't. On the way to the hospital and throughout my stay there, I immediately (intuitively) recognized my powerlessness (Step 1), I turned my will and my life over to the care of my Higher Power (Step 3), and I meditated the best I could before, during and after my surgical procedure and regularly while I was in the hospital (Step 11). And I had the joyous opportunity to work the 12ᵗʰ Step by practicing the principles at the hospital. I was able to be kind, loving and grateful to the medical personnel, friends and loved ones who surrounded me. My defensive shields were down enough for me to accept the generous help lovingly and graciously offered. This was my Higher Power doing for me what I could not do for myself. I believe the Program's recovery process had metaphorically finally softened my heart to the point that the "armor" around my heart finally cracked.

11ᵗʰ Step meditation is the golden clasp that holds the diamond necklace of the Program together. Will you use it? The rest is up to you. I leave you with a traditional encouragement about meditation:

Now is the time to do as you think fit.

Meditation reveals the hidden jewel of our recovery.

> There once was a man who fell into a drunken sleep. His kind friend stayed with the man as long as he could, but after a while the friend had to go on about his way. The friend was concerned that the drunken man had no money and would fall on hard times, so he hid a jewel in the drunken man's clothes.

> When the drunken man awoke, he lived in poverty and hunger, unaware that his old friend had placed a jewel in his clothes. A long time passed, when the two men happened to meet one day in a distant place. The kind friend could not understand why the man was poor and hungry. He asked what had happened to the jewel. The poor man replied, "I didn't know it was there. I didn't know to look."

Endnotes

1   Adapted from Ernest Kurtz and Katherine Ketcham, The Spirituality of
    Imperfection: Storytelling and the Journey to Wholeness (Bantam Books, 1994),
    pp.86-87

2   Alcoholics Anonymous: The Story of How Many Thousands of Men &
    Women Have Recovered from Alcoholism, (Alcoholics Anonymous World
    Services, Inc., 3rd edition 1976), p. 69

3   Twelve Steps and Twelve Traditions (Alcoholics Anonymous World Services,
    Inc., 1981), p. 99

4   Joseph Goldstein, Insight Meditation: The Practice of Freedom, (Shambhala,
    1993), p. 123

5   Jon Kabat-Zinn, Wherever You Go, There You Are: Mindfulness Meditation in
    Everyday Life (Hyperion, 1994), p. 35

6   Joseph Goldstein, To Open, To Balance, To Explore, quoted in Jean Smith
    (editor), Breath Sweeps Mind: A First Guide to Meditation Practice (Riverhead
    Books, 1998), p. 71

7   Kabat-Zinn , Wherever You Go, There You Are, p. 14

8   Kabat-Zinn, Wherever You Go, There You Are, p. 11

9   Kabat-Zinn, Wherever You Go, There You Are, p. 6

10 Jack Kornfield, The Art of Awakening, quoted in Jean Smith (editor), Breath
    Sweeps Mind, p. 17

11 Jack Kornfield and Paul Breiter, A Still Forest Pool: The Insight Meditation of
    Achaan Chah (Theosophical Publishing House, 1985), pp. 150-151

12 Kornfield and Breiter, A Still Forest Pool, pp. 157

13 Ajahn Sumedo, The Mind and the Way: Buddhist Reflections on Life (Wisdom
    Publications, 1995), p. 44

14 Charlotte Joko Beck, Nothing Special: Living Zen (Harper San Francisco,
    1993), p.87

15 Dennis Genpo Merzel, The Eye Never Sleeps: Striking to the Heart of Zen
    (Shambhala 1991), p. 19

16 From Insight Meditation Society, Barre, Massachusetts

17 Adapted from Kurtz and Ketcham, The Spirituality of Imperfection, p. 15

18   Stephen Batchelor, The Faith to Doubt: Glimpses of Buddhist Uncertainty (Parallax Press, 1990), p. 31

19   Cheri Huber, Trying to be Human (Present Perfect Books, 1995), p. 9

20   Mark Epstein, M.D., Thoughts Without a Thinker: Psychotherapy from a Buddhist Perspective (BasicBooks, 1995), p. 61

21   Alcoholics Anonymous, p. 62

22   Alan Watts, Talking Zen (Weatherhill, 1994), p. 33 (quoting Chuang Tzu)

23   Pema Chödrön, When Things Fall Apart (Shambhala 1997), pp. 54-55

24   Adapted from Kurtz and Ketcham, The Spirituality of Imperfection, p. 107

25   Epstein, Thoughts Without a Thinker, pp. 3-4

26   Huber, The Perils and Pitfalls of Practice, p. 113

27   Kornfield, A Path with Heart, p. 57

28   Adapted from William Hart, The Art of Living: Vipassana Meditation as Taught by S.N. Goenka (Harper San Francisco, 1987), pp 68-69

29   Robert Aitken, Taking the Path of Zen (North Point Press, 1982), p. 14

30   Shunryu Suzuki, Zen Mind, Beginner's Mind: Informal Talks on Zen Meditation and Practice (John Weatherhill, Inc. 1970), p.26

31   Kornfield, A Path with Heart, p. 59

32   Sylvia Boorstein, It's Easier Than You Think: The Buddhist Way to Happiness (Harper San Francisco, 1995), p. 73

33   Cheri Huber, Turning Toward Happiness: Conversations with a Zen Teacher and Her Students (Present Perfect Books, 1991), p. 36

34   Chögyam Trungpa, Cutting Through Spiritual Materialism (Shambhala 1973), p. 4

35   Thich Nhat Hanh, Zen Keys (Doubleday, 1974), p. 44

36   Adapted from Watts, Talking Zen, p. 175

37   Robert Aitken, Encouraging Words: Zen Buddhist Teachings for Western Students, (Pantheon, 1993), p 46

38   Kornfield, A Path with Heart, p. 58

39   Cooper, The Heart of Stillness, p. 94

40   Pema Chödrön, Start Where You Are: A Guide to Compassionate Living (Shambhala, 1994), p. 68

41   Epstein, Thoughts Without A Thinker, p. 110

42   Goldstein, Insight Meditation, p. 113

43   Kurtz and Ketcham, The Spirituality of Imperfection, p 159

44   Cooper, The Heart of Stillness, p. 143

45   Batchelor, Buddhism Without Beliefs, p. 6

46   Cooper, The Heart of Stillness, p. 78

47   Huber, Trying to Be Human, p. 20

48   Epstein, Thoughts Without a Thinker, p. 207

49 Chödrön, When Things Fall Apart, p.22

50 Charlotte Joko Beck, Everyday Zen: Love and Work (Harper San Francisco, 1989), p. 3

51 quoting Mumon, Lenore Friedman, Meetings with Remarkable Women: Buddhist Teachers in America (Shambhala, 1987), p. 90

52 Cooper, The Heart of Stillness, p. 92

53 Kyogen Carlson, Zen in the American Grain: Discovering the Teachings at Home (Station Hill, 1994), p.110

54 Adapted from the Majjhima Nikaya

55 Huang Po, quoted in Hagen, Buddhism Plain and Simple, p. 148

56 Trungpa, Cutting Through Spiritual Materialism, p. 131

57 Huber, Trying to Be Human, p. 57

58 Sosan Zenji, Hsin Hsin Ming, based on a translation from the Chinese by Richard B. Clarke, modified by Dennis Genpo Merzel, The Eye Never Sleeps, p. 126

59 Kurtz and Ketcham, The Spirituality of Imperfection, p. 30, quoting Saint Gregory of Nyssa.

60 Suzuki, Zen Mind, Beginner's Mind, p. 21

61 Venerable Henepola Gunaratara, Mindfulness in Plain English (Wisdom Publications, 1991), p. 12

62 Adapted from "A Cup of Tea" compiled by Paul Reps, Zen Flesh, Zen Bones: A Collection of Zen and Pre-Zen Writings (Anchor, 1961, 1989), p. 5

63 Kurtz and Ketcham, The Spirituality of Imperfection, p. 200

64 Watts, Talking Zen, p. 139

65 Huber, The Perils and Pitfalls of Practice, p. 105

66 Adapted from the Yogacara Bhumi Sutra, translated by Arthur Waley

67 Adapted from "Muddy Road," Reps, Zen Flesh, Zen Bones, p.18

68 Huber, Turning Toward Happiness, p. 14

69 Huber, Trying to Be Human, p. 49

70 Kornfield, A Path with Heart, p. 193

71 Adapted from "Parable of the Mustard Seed," Teachings of the Buddha, Jack Kornfield and Gil Fronsdal (editors) (Shambhala 1996), pp. 35-37

72 Kabat-Zinn, Wherever You Go, There You Are, p. xiii

73 Chödrön, When Things Fall Apart, p.2

74 Thich Nhat Hanh, The Miracle of Mindfulness (Beacon Press, 1975), p. 4

75 Kurtz and Ketcham, The Spirituality of Imperfection, pp. 36-37

76 Trungpa, Cutting Through Spiritual Materialism, p. 159

77 Rosenberg, Breath by Breath, p. 60

78 Cheri Huber, The Key and the Name of the Key is Willingness (1984), p. 31

79 Carlson, Zen in the American Grain, p. 65

80   Goldstein, Insight Meditation, p. 123

81   Adapted from "A Parable" compiled by Paul Reps, Zen Flesh, Zen Bones, pp. 22-23

82   Huber, Trying to Be Human, p. 43

83   Chödrön, Start Where You Are, p 6

84   Huber, Trying to Be Human, p. 48

85   Kurtz and Ketcham, The Spirituality of Imperfection, p. 185

86   Alcoholics Anonymous, p. 84

87   Chödrön, Start Where You Are, p. 128

88   Mel Ash, The Zen of Recovery (Jeremy P. Tarcher/Perigree Books, 1993), p. 78

89   Kornfield, A Path with Heart, op. cit , p. 279

90   Beck, Nothing Special, p.7

91   Chödrön, When Things Fall Apart, p. 35

92   Adapted from Hart, The Art of Living, pp 42-43

93   Hanh, Zen Keys, p. 5

94   Chödrön, When Things Fall Apart, pp. 78-79.

95   Chödrön, When Things Fall Apart, p. 87

96   Chödrön, Start Where You Are, p.104

97   Adapted from Kurtz and Ketcham, The Spirituality of Imperfection, pp. 9-10

98   Cooper, The Heart of Stillness, p. 18

99   Chödrön, When Things Fall Apart, p. 104

100   Kornfield, A Path with Heart, p. 33

101   Chödrön, When Things Fall Apart, p. 2

102   Chödrön, When Things Dallas Apart, p. 127

103   Lao-tzu, Tao Te Ching, quoted in Kabat-Zinn, Wherever You Go, There You Are, p. 51

104   Huber, Trying to Be Human, p. 15

105   Chödrön, When Things Fall Apart, p. 16

106   Beck, Nothing Special: Living Zen, p. 114

107   Adapted from Chödrön, Start Where You Are, p. 57

108   Chödrön, When Things Fall Apart, p. 65

109   Chödrön, When Things Fall Apart, p. 123

110   Chödrön, Start Where You Are, p. 77

111   Adapted from Hagen, Buddhism Plain and Simple, p. 17

112   Joseph Goldstein, The Experience of Insight: A Simple and Direct Guide to Buddhist Meditation (Shambhala, 1976), p. 159

113   Adapted from Richard McClean, Zen Fables for Today: Timeless Stories Inspired by the Zen Masters (Avon, 1998), p. 75

About the Author

 Laurence Sanger is a veteran of 12-Step Programs and a 21-year meditation practitioner. An attorney in private practice, he is also the business manager of Insights Collaborative Therapy Group, a psychotherapy practice owned by his wife, Mary. He also teaches meditation classes and has lectured on Buddhist psychology. Laurence lives in Dallas, Texas, with Mary, and their wonder dog, Spanky.

Made in the USA
Monee, IL
14 May 2021

68554167R00109